Globalisation and HR

Hilary Harris

Chris Brewster

Paul Sparrow

The Chartered Institute of Personnel and Development is the leading publisher of books and reports for personnel and training professionals, students, and all those concerned with the effective management and development of people at work. For full details of all our titles, please contact the Publishing Department:

Tel: 020 8263 3387
Fax: 020 8263 3850

E-mail: publish@cipd.co.uk

The catalogue of all CIPD titles can be viewed on the CIPD website:
www.cipd.co.uk/publications

Globalisation and HR

A literature review

Dr Hilary Harris
Cranfield University School of Management

Professor Chris Brewster
South Bank University

Professor Paul Sparrow
Manchester Business School

© Chartered Institute of Personnel and Development 2001

First published 2001

Cover design by Curve
Designed and typeset by Beacon GDT
Printed in Great Britain by Short Run Press

British Library Cataloguing in Publication Data
A catalogue record for this book is available from the British Library

ISBN 0 85292 946 3

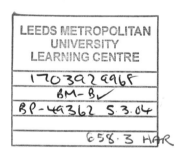

Chartered Institute of Personnel and Development,
CIPD House, Camp Road, London SW19 4UX

Tel: 020 8971 9000
Fax: 020 8263 3333
Website: www.cipd.co.uk

Incorporated by Royal Charter. Registered charity no. 1079797.

Contents

Foreword

We are all very aware that today's business world is rapidly changing. It is becoming increasingly global and boundaries are rapidly disappearing due to technological advancements, greater mobility of people, higher education levels and the driving need by business to be cost-effective. Movement towards vertical business structures is increasing and the advent of complex matrix ways of working is becoming part of the tapestry of today's business world. Globalisation is now an accepted way of life, the pace of change is increasing in leaps and bounds and the business world demands continuing innovation. Management of change and ways to support business in this new environment has become a fundamental prerequisite for HR management.

The CIPD has been very aware of the dramatic impact all of these changes are having on the people management profession and has implemented a major research project to draw together the different threads of what is known practically and academically in the fields of international HR management. The project will also provide a detailed and practical analysis of what is needed to be successful in terms of skills and experience to equip people management and development professionals to operate effectively in a globalised environment through effective knowledge development and sharing. One key part of this research is to pull together and evaluate what available literature has been published on international HR management, and this is presented here.

The literature review has been authored by Professor Chris Brewster of South Bank University (formerly of Cranfield University School of Management), Dr Hilary Harris of Cranfield University School of Management and Paul Sparrow of Manchester Business School (formerly of Sheffield University Management School). Each is an expert in international and global human resources management and they have skilfully woven together in a practical and effective manner the major aspects that should be the concern of any HR professional working in a global environment.

The authors have clearly set out in a coherent fashion the major areas that have been addressed by the publishers of the literature. People management professionals and others with an interest in the impact of the globalisation of business on HR have been provided with an analysis of what are the key challenges, the major milestones, the linkages and how thinking has evolved and will continue to evolve for what faces the future of HR in the global world.

Peter Squire
CIPD Vice-President International

Executive summary

- Globalisation of business is driving the need for people management (PM) professionals in small to medium-sized enterprises (SMEs) as well as multinationals (MNEs) to adopt an international orientation in their functional activities.

- The literature on international HRM is extensive but fragmented. Three main approaches to international HRM have been taken by researchers: a cross-cultural management approach, a comparative HR approach and the study of HRM in MNEs.

- Organisations adopting a structure that emphasises strong central control will adopt an ethnocentric attitude to staffing and HR policy and practice. This approach favours the use of headquarters expatriates and high standardisation of all HR policies and practices.

- Organisations that are striving to be truly global in their scope will adopt a geocentric attitude to staffing and HR policy. This approach ignores nationality in favour of ability and integrates HR policies and practices.

- One of the critical challenges facing the global PM professional is the need to balance the conflicting demands of global standardisation and local differentiation: the 'global v local' dilemma.

- The additional complexities of managing an international workforce call for a different mindset and different skills for practitioners.

- Global PM professionals will need greater competence in interpersonal skills, influencing and negotiating, analytical and conceptual abilities, and strategic thinking. They will also need a broader base of knowledge in areas such as international business, finance, labour legislation and local labour markets, and national cultural differences.

- A critical challenge for global PM professionals is the ability to take a more strategic approach to the management of international workers. This will involve an assessment of the appropriate type of assignment to deliver organisational goals. It will also include a holistic approach to the management of all stages of the assignment.

- Little research has been carried out to date on measuring the effectiveness of the global PM function. In terms of added value, key contributions are seen to be:

  – developing global leadership through cross-cultural assignments

  – making human resources a strategic partner in global business

  – ensuring flexibility in all human resource programmes and processes.

- Measuring the value of international assignments will enable organisations to make informed strategic decisions on international staffing configurations.

- Outsourcing of international assignment administration and the introduction of shared services models means that global PM professionals need to position their activities at the top end of the value chain to be seen as a true strategic partner in global organisations.

1 | Introduction

Globalisation: implications for practitioners

The need for people management (PM) professionals to adopt an increasingly international orientation in their functional activities is widely acknowledged. This new focus applies not just to people working in multinational enterprises (MNEs), but also to many in small to medium-sized enterprises (SMEs). The additional complexities of managing an international workforce call for a different mindset and different skills for practitioners.

Any review of world events over the past 10 years will emphasise the essentially unpredictable and rapidly changing nature of political, economic and social upheavals. Peter Vaill, writing in 1989, used the metaphor of 'permanent white water' to describe the nature of doing business in the latter part of the twentieth century.

Most managers are taught to think of themselves as paddling their canoes on calm, still lakes... Sure there will be temporary disruptions during changes of various sorts – periods when they will have to shoot the rapids in their canoes – but the disruptions will be temporary, and when things settle back down, they'll be back in a calm, still lake mode. But it has been my experience – that you never get out of the rapids!

Whilst managers in organisations working in a single-country environment are still subject to the twists and turns of external events, the manager working in an international environment must try to assess the impact of multi-country, regional and global trends. Hardly surprisingly, choices in this context become complex and ambiguous. For example, a human resource manager in a domestically based company taking its first steps on the road to internationalisation will probably ponder the following questions:

◘ Do we have a strategy for becoming an international firm?

◘ What type of managers shall we need to be successful?

◘ How shall we choose whether to send expatriates or use locals?

◘ Can we have standard policies and practices worldwide?

◘ What will be the impact of local cultural norms on our ways of working?

◘ How do we manage international moves?

◘ How do we source/reward/manage performance globally?

◘ What constraints shall we face through local labour legislation and unions?

◘ What type of employee representation will be appropriate?

◘ How do we manage knowledge across geographical and cultural distance?

An experienced PM specialist in a domestic situation would have few problems creating and implementing an HR strategy for a greenfield site. Both the Professional Qualification Scheme of the CIPD and many academic courses equip practitioners with the knowledge and tools to help shape and deliver corporate strategy. The PM professional working in an international context does not, however, have such a clear path to proficiency. We would argue that these individuals need greater competence in:

'There is a clear need...to pull together the disparate strands of research in this area to provide an overview of the major elements affecting HR policy and practice choice in an international environment.'

- interpersonal skills (especially cultural empathy)
- influencing and negotiating skills
- analytical and conceptual abilities
- strategic thinking.

They will also need a broader base of knowledge in such areas as:

- international business
- international finance
- international labour legislation
- local labour markets
- cultural differences
- international compensation and benefits.

Taking a stakeholder perspective, the international PM professional again needs to be able to manage multiple relationships. For instance, a manager working within a European context will need to consider the perspectives of the following stakeholders:

- headquarters and subsidiary managers
- headquarters and subsidiary employees
- national and European-level trade unions
- national and European-level legislative bodies
- national and European-level government officials
- local and regional communities.

It is evident, therefore, that the set of competencies required of an international PM practitioner is significantly different from that of their domestically based colleagues. There is a clear need, however, to pull together the disparate strands of research in this area to provide an overview of the major elements affecting HR policy and practice choice in an international environment. The CIPD has begun this process with a number of publications in the area of comparative and international HRM. The recent CIPD book *The Global HR Manager* (Joynt and Morton 1999) is an example.

This report attempts to address this need by outlining the major influences on human resource policy and practice for organisations working across borders; the impact of this for the role of the international PM professional; ways in which we can monitor the effectiveness of PM interventions in a global environment; and questions that practitioners and researchers need to address about the impact of globalisation for the business role of PM professionals.

The research addresses the following questions:

1 What business models are driving the international HR agenda? What are the links to business strategy?

2 Is there a difference between international HRM and HRM in a domestic context? Does international HRM influence the business agenda more than domestic HRM?

3 What is the impact of international HRM on organisational effectiveness?

4 How effective and important for business is the role of the international personnel and development manager?

5 What are the keys to success in international HRM?

6 What are the different HR models of organisation being used, identifying best practice to support vertical global/international/regional businesses?

7 What diagnostic frameworks and processes can be defined to help international personnel and development managers make informed choices from the existing theoretical contingency frameworks and the new empirical evidence, which will be produced by this study?

The aims of the proposed research are intended to produce a coherent package of research. They are as follows:

◻ to report on the business development trends shaping the international HRM agenda

◻ to establish a knowledge base to guide the professional development of international people management specialists based on a range of relevant literature

◻ to gain empirical evidence of current configurations of international HR practices and to assess the impact of international HR on organisational effectiveness

◻ to look in more depth at the role of people management specialists in a variety of international management contexts

◻ to identify leading-edge and innovative business cases that tap a wide range of organisational contexts that dictate an international role for people management specialists

◻ to establish the limits to international convergence of HR policy and practice at the individual, organisational and national level.

Aims and structure of the report

The aim of this report is to evaluate critically the available literature on international HRM (IHRM). It will bring together the various strands of research in this area to provide an overview of the major elements affecting PM policy and practice choice in an international environment. Specifically, the report addresses:

◻ the three main approaches to IHRM in the literature

    – a cross-cultural management approach examining human behaviour in organisations from an international perspective

    – a comparative HRM approach seeking to describe, compare and analyse HRM systems in various countries

    – a third approach that focuses on aspects of HRM in multinational firms

◻ the nature of the role of the global PM professional and how this differs from a domestically based practitioner

◻ the developing role of the global PM professional within a context of the changing nature of international operations and international workers

◻ the extent to which the business contribution of PM professionals can be measured in a global environment.

2 | Approaches to IHRM: cross-cultural management

☑ **Evidence from cross-cultural researchers indicates significant differences in work values and attitudes at a national level.**

☑ **PM professionals in global organisations may need to alter policies and practices to adapt to national cultural differences.**

☑ **Culture is dynamic and reported groupings of countries into cultural clusters may need to be reassessed.**

A key factor in the increasing internationalisation of employment is that there are cultural differences between nations: differences in national values and attitude systems. For instance, most managers in the UK are aware that the Japanese do things differently, particularly in the way they manage their people. The great success of Japanese industry in the 1980s led to a rush amongst US and UK managers to adopt Japanese management practices such as quality circles. All too often, the results were disappointing as these managers had failed to recognise that the success of the practices in Japan was inextricably related to societal norms reinforcing a collectivist approach to work and life. Even when managers are aware of differences, they are often not clear about the differences in any detail. This can lead to inaccurate stereotyping. Another complicating factor when working across cultures is that although we are aware of differences at a national level in attitudes and value systems, we are also aware that every individual is different. So despite the evidence, it is likely that we may come across an autocratic Swedish manager, a disorganised German technician and a laid-back US executive. The problem of trying to align individual personality traits with national cultural patterns is one that is still being worked on by researchers. What is clear from research to date is that there is value in exploring the impact of national cultures on doing business in different situations. It is, however, important to be clear about our

definitions and levels of analysis to avoid confusion between individual and national cultural level differences.

Definitions

There are many definitions of culture, but the term usually refers to a shaping process. For a culture to exist, members of a group or society must share a distinct way of life with common values, attitudes and behaviours that are transmitted over time in a gradual yet dynamic process. Hofstede's (1980) definition of culture is widely quoted. He argues that culture is:

The collective programming of the mind which distinguishes the members of one human group from another – the interactive aggregate of common characteristics that influences a human group's response to its environment.

We can see from this that there can be many forms of culture: organisational, professional, ethnic, religious, regional, as well as national. Our focus here is on national culture.

For the purposes of this report, therefore, the word 'culture' will be taken to mean something that:

☑ is shared by almost all members of a group

'What is clear ... is that there is value in exploring the impact of national cultures on doing business in different situations.'

◘ is passed on from the older or more senior members to the younger or subordinate members

◘ shapes our perception of the world and of people's behaviour (eg morals, laws and customs).

As such, culture is formed by and linked to a whole series of societal artefacts (see Figure 1).

Elements of culture

The basic elements making up national-level cultures were seen by anthropologists Kluckholn and Strodtbeck (1961) to lie in the responses that nations make in relation to six fundamental questions:

◘ Who are we?

◘ How do we relate to the world?

Figure 1 | The composition of culture

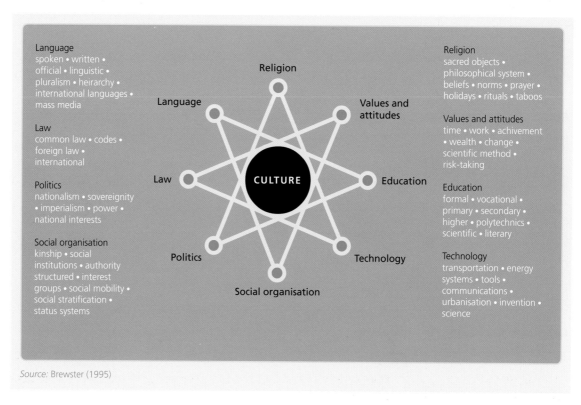

Language
spoken • written • official • linguistic • pluralism • heirarchy • international languages • mass media

Law
common law • codes • foreign law • international

Politics
nationalism • sovereignity • imperialism • power • national interests

Social organisation
kinship • social institutions • authority structured • interest groups • social mobility • social stratification • status systems

Religion
sacred objects • philosophical system • beliefs • norms • prayer • holidays • rituals • taboos

Values and attitudes
time • work • achivement • wealth • change • scientific method • risk-taking

Education
formal • vocational • primary • secondary • higher • polytechnics • scientific • literary

Technology
transportation • energy systems • tools • communications • urbanisation • invention • science

Religion — Language — Values and attitudes — Law — CULTURE — Education — Politics — Technology — Social organisation

Source: Brewster (1995)

- How do we relate to each other?

- What do we do?

- How do we think about time?

- How do we think about space?

Who are we?

How does a society conceive of people's qualities as individuals? If societies believe that people are basically good, they will try to exercise social control through praise and encouragement. If people are seen as fundamentally bad, control will be exercised via rules, laws and policing. If societies see people as capable of being changed, they will prefer reform to punishment.

How do we relate to the world?

How important is nature and the environment in our thinking? And how do we conceive of nature? Some societies feel that it is important to fit in with the world and accept it, as in the Arabic expression 'inshallah' or 'God willing'. In contrast, countries like the USA expect to overcome the constraints imposed by the environment. This can be translated in the business world into attempts to control markets and consumer tastes.

How do we relate to each other?

Do we think of ourselves as individuals or as members of a group? In many Western cultures we are happy to live far from members of our family and to have non-emotional links with the organisations we work for. In contrast, members of collectivist societies expect support and loyalty to the extended family. In the business world, this aspect of culture affects the extent to which

people are happy with individual leadership, individual responsibility and target-setting, or whether they prefer group working and shared responsibility.

What do we do?

Is our purpose in life to do things, to achieve success, or is our purpose to enjoy what is happening to us? Is our primary orientation *action*, or *being*? Managers from action-oriented countries are more likely to suffer stress and work longer hours.

How do we think about time?

In a cultural sense, time has two elements: locus and speed. In Western societies time moves in one direction, with the locus of attention on the future. In other societies, such as some Pacific islands, all parts of time are connected. The past is as important as the present, with the future being seen as less important. In a business context, Western societies see time as a commodity to be managed and used well. Other societies have a more relaxed approach to the timing of things, causing problems with perceptions of correct business conduct.

How do we think about space?

The amount of space we feel we need varies around the world. In the Northern Hemisphere, the further west you go, the larger the rooms and offices tend to be. Physical space between people is also culturally determined. In Arab societies it is common to stand close to the person one is talking to. This is not the case for the British, who prefer to stand at an arm's distance away from the person they are talking to. The use of space in organisations gives clues as to the status of the

> 'Where individualism is high...people are expected to take care of themselves...In collectivist societies...the allegiance of an individual is to a broader group.'

person occupying the area, but these need to be interpreted from a cultural perspective.

Research into national cultural differences

These fundamental questions are reflected in some of the subsequent research into national cultural differences. Three European researchers have been particularly influential in this respect.

Andre Laurent (1986) studied the responses that management students from different countries gave to a series of statements about managerial styles. He was able to show significant national differences. For instance, some nationalities were much more likely than others to assume that a manager should have the answers to any questions that subordinates might ask. Equally some nationalities more than others saw reasons for organisational hierarchy as connected with knowing who has authority over whom. Laurent classified the nationalities concerned according to separate theories of organisations: as political systems, as authority systems, as role-formalisation systems and as hierarchical-relationship systems.

One of the most influential pieces of research in relation to national cultures is the work of Hofstede (1980; 1991). Hofstede analysed survey data from 116,000 employees of IBM in 48 different countries. The results of his analysis showed that nationality did affect many cultural assumptions and business practices. Although Hofstede's work is now quite dated and questions have been raised about several features of his methodology, his framework is widely used by researchers and practitioners in the field of intercultural management. Hofstede found that the differences in responses could be explained by four main factors:

- power distance

- uncertainty avoidance

- individualism

- masculinity.

Power distance

This relates to the extent to which societies accept that power in institutions and organisations is and should be distributed unequally. In organisational terms, this relates to the centralisation of authority and the degree of autocratic leadership. Societies with 'high power distance' scores will be reflected in hierarchical organisations where it is felt to be right that the superior is seen to be more powerful than subordinates. Examples of countries with high power distance scores are France, Greece, Singapore and the Philippines. In contrast, countries with low power distance scores, such as Britain, Sweden and New Zealand, favour a more democratic style of management and flatter organisational structures.

Uncertainty avoidance

This dimension refers to the degree to which societies feel threatened by ambiguous situations and the extent to which they try to avoid uncertain situations. In countries with high uncertainty avoidance, such as Austria, organisations will adopt strong bureaucracies and career stability and generally discourage risk-taking activities. Countries such as Sweden, Britain and Norway, which exhibit low uncertainty avoidance, will adopt more flexible structures and encourage more diverse views.

Individualism

The individualism–collectivist continuum reflects the extent to which individuals are integrated into groups. Where individualism is high, for example in the USA, people are expected to take care of themselves and their immediate family only. In collectivist societies such as Japan, however, the allegiance of an individual is to a broader group. Whereas in individualist societies the emphasis for individuals within organisations is to gain self-respect and personal achievement, in collectivist societies the focus is on fitting in harmoniously and face-saving.

Masculinity

The final dimension has now been relabelled by Hofstede as 'quality of life'. This dimension measures the extent to which the dominant values are (in Hofstede's terms) 'male' – values such as assertiveness, the acquisition of money and goods, and not caring for others. Gender roles are more rigidly defined in masculine societies than in 'feminine' societies. The most masculine countries in Hofstede's framework are Japan and Austria, with the USA falling into this category. In contrast, the Scandinavian countries fall into the feminine category, with more emphasis on work–life balance.

The final piece of research was carried out by Trompenaars (1993). He administered research questionnaires to over 15,000 managers from 28 countries. He found seven dimensions of difference as follows:

1 *Universalism v particularism* – this measures the extent to which people believe that general principles are more, or less, important than unique circumstances and relationships. In business contexts this relates to the need for detailed contracts or a relationship of trust.

2 *Specific v diffuse* – how much societies prefer to deal with situations or problems by breaking them down into components, as opposed to dealing with them holistically.

3 *Individualism v communitarianism* – similar to Hofstede's individualism dimension.

4 *Inner-directed v outer-directed* – the extent to which it is acceptable to follow one's own views rather than adapt to the majority.

5 *Time as sequence v time as synchronisation* – see discussion of time in Kluckholn and Strodtbeck section (page 7).

6 *Achievement v ascription* – how power and status are seen to be allocated in a society – whether it is given or can be given.

7 *Equality v hierarchy* – similar to Hofstede's power distance dimension.

A great deal of research activity has focused on the extent to which aspects of business practices in any particular country are *emic* (ie culture-specific aspects of concepts or behaviour) or *etic* (ie culture-common aspects). Certain researchers argue that organisations are essentially 'culture free' (Lammers and Hickson 1979) and that technology (Child 1981) and strategic orientation (Miles and Snow 1986) override differences in national context, leading to a global standardisation of management practices. On the other hand, the work of cross-cultural researchers such as Hofstede and Trompenaars would appear to demonstrate that organisations are 'culture bound' and that management practices are heavily influenced by collectively shared values and belief systems. Rosenzweig and Nohria (1994) argued that HR is the area of management most likely to be subject to national differences.

Implications for HRM practices

The implications for HRM practices arising from societies' differential cultural positioning are extensive and have been documented by many writers. Schneider (1988) argues that national cultural differences will affect most HR practices, such as planning and staffing, appraisal and compensation, and selection and socialisation. Sparrow and Hiltrop (1994) used the results of a worldwide survey by Towers Perrin to explore how different cultural groupings of countries might affect usage of a range of HRM variables. They found that the survey data identified an Anglo-Saxon grouping composed of Australia, Canada, the UK and the USA; three cultural islands (France, South Korea and Japan) and a further grouping of cultural allies comprising the South American or Latin countries of Brazil, Mexico and Argentina. The nature of the differences between the cultural clusters were analysed across five major HRM variables:

◘ culture change

  – promoting an empowerment culture

  – promoting diversity and an equality culture

◘ organisation structure and control variables

  – emphasis on flexible organisation/work practices

  – emphasis on centralisation and vertical hierarchy

  – emphasis on utilising IT to structure the organisation

  – emphasis on horizontal management

◘ performance/process management variables

  – emphasis on measuring and promoting customer service

  – emphasis on rewarding innovation/ creativity

  – link between pay and individual performance

  – shared benefits, risks and pay for performance

◘ resourcing variables

  – emphasis on external resourcing

  – emphasis on internal resourcing – training and careers

  – emphasis on internal resourcing – managing outflows

◘ communication/corporate responsibility variables

  – emphasis on communication

  – emphasis on corporate responsibility.

The researchers found significant differences between cultural groupings on items within the culture change, organisation structure and performance management variables. For instance, Japan scored significantly lower on 'promoting an empowerment culture' compared to the Anglo-American representative USA and the Latin American representative Brazil. On the structuring items, the USA scored significantly higher on 'emphasis on work practices' compared to France and Brazil. Few differences were found, however, within the resourcing and communication and corporate responsibility variables. Other studies have found societies clustering in very different ways.

This chapter has demonstrated that a significant difference for people management professionals working in an international context is the need to consider national cultural differences (and potentially other significant cultural groupings) when designing and implementing HR policy and practice. Such a finding questions the applicability of the universalist approach advocated by the majority of US writers on HRM. The next chapter examines research into comparative HRM, which reinforces the need for a contextualist approach to HRM to deliver effective international HR strategy.

3 | Approaches to IHRM: comparative HR research

☑ **The universalist paradigm assumes a common objective and approach to HRM and has been the underlying theme of US writers on strategic HRM.**

☑ **A contextualist approach acknowledges the impact of broader societal and governmental forces in shaping the nature of HRM in each country.**

☑ **Evidence from comparative research into PM argues against the 'one best way' approach usually recommended by US authors.**

The importance of considering national cultural differences when implementing IHRM policies and practices is underlined by international comparative research. This highlights the fact that theories of management have tended to be constructed in one country (typically the USA, but theories from other countries show the same cultural specificity – the Weber 'bureaucratic' approach in Germany; the 'professional management' discipline of Fayol in France, etc). More recently, there has been a reaction to the dominant US model with attempts to construct other approaches, still claimed as universally applicable, in Germany (Kern and Schumann 1984) and Sweden (Berggren 1992). It has been suggested that other European researchers who argue for nationally distinct approaches to organisation, for example Lane (1989), show an implicit tendency to assume that one model, generally the German one here, is superior. This approach can also be seen in some US writers who have looked outside their own country and elevated, for example, the Japanese approach (Ouchi 1981; Pascale and Athos 1982) as a model towards which organisations and nations should aspire.

Not surprisingly, there has been a related tendency for HR policies and practices to be designed in one country and transplanted into another. This ignores the fact that the thinking and assumptions behind the behavioural implications of these practices are taken from one national context, one national culture. As mentioned earlier, this can be problematic given that knowledge of societies, of their language(s), their concepts, their values, their culture, is fundamental to understanding the behaviour of people within employing organisations. By its nature, people management is the area of management that is most influenced by the local national environment.

This problem relates to a fundamental division between two approaches to research and thinking in the field of HRM. Two research paradigms can be identified: the universalist and the contextual (or comparative).

The universalist paradigm

Much of the research emanating from the USA in the field of HRM, and particularly strategic HRM, assumes a universalist paradigm (for example, Ulrich 1987; Wright and McMahan 1992). That is to say, there is an assumption that the purpose of strategic HRM is to improve the way that human resources are managed strategically within organisations, with the ultimate aim of improving organisational performance (Huselid 1995). Further, it is implicit that this objective will apply in all cases. The limitation of this approach is that it ignores other levels and stakeholders (apart from customers and shareholders) in the outcomes of HRM.

' ...there has been a...tendency for HR policies and practices to be designed in one country and transplanted into another.'

The contextualist or comparative paradigm

In contrast, the contextual paradigm assumes that societies, governments or regions can have strategic HRM as well as firms. At the level of the organisation, the overall strategy and objectives are not necessarily assumed to be 'good', either for the organisation or society. There is also an acknowledgement of differing interest groups within organisations. The focus here is on external factors as well as the actions of management within an organisation. Hence it explores the importance on HR policy and practice within individual organisations of such factors as:

◘ culture

◘ ownership structures

◘ labour markets

◘ the role of the state

◘ trade union organisation.

In Europe, many management researchers find the universalist paradigm ironically excludes much of the work of HR specialists. Examples include:

◘ compliance

◘ equal opportunities

◘ trade union relationships

◘ dealing with local government.

In addition, the universalist paradigm operates only at the level of the organisation. This is not helpful in Europe, where significant HR legislation and policy is enacted at EU level (eg freedom of movement, employment and remuneration, equal treatment) as well as those of particular countries or sectors (Brewster *et al* 1996; Sparrow and Hiltrop 1994).

One of the most extensive research studies into comparative HR practices is the ongoing Cranet-E Project co-ordinated by Cranfield School of Management (see for example Brewster *et al* 2000). This is a triennial survey of organisational policies and practices in human resource management, originally across Europe and now global. The findings from the survey clearly demonstrate significant differences in HR policy and practice at a national level amongst the participating countries.

One of the key influencing factors is the regulatory framework surrounding the employment relationship, which is far more extensive in European countries than in the USA. Although Europe is unique in the world in having 15 countries committed to a supranational level of legislation, there are many areas of difference at national level. These can include:

◘ the regulation of recruitment and dismissal

◘ the formalisation of educational certification

◘ the industrial relations framework.

Other areas of difference include (Brewster and Bournois 1991):

◘ legislative requirements on pay, hours of work and forms of employment contract

◘ rights to trade union representation

'Variations in legislative frameworks result from differing social, economic, cultural and political contexts...These...lead to differences in policy and practice in almost all areas of HRM.'

◘ requirements to establish and operate consultation and co-determination arrangements.

The extent to which HR practices and policies can be standardised across countries is also highly influenced by the social and welfare context. Although the EU has seen attempts to co-ordinate policy in many social and legislative areas, major differences still exist, particularly in relation to differing taxation and social security systems. These will affect not only the potential mobility of employees across national boundaries, but also the extent to which common HR practices can be implemented. For example, in Belgium, it has been argued that the taxation system blunts the impact of incentives and fringe benefits (Sels 1992) and thereby limits the use of rewards as an integrating mechanism for HRM or the adoption of performance management techniques.

Variations in legislative frameworks result from differing social, economic, cultural and political contexts in individual nation states. These in turn lead to differences in policy and practice in almost all areas of HRM. For instance in France, 90 per cent of organisations use graphology as a shortlisting technique in selection, a practice that would be derided as a gimmick in the UK.

A related aspect in determining the extent to which HR practices can be transferred between countries is the extent of organisational autonomy from the state. The USA and continental Europe show very different orientations here. The relationship between organisations and the state in the USA is characterised by:

◘ high autonomy

◘ low levels of industrial support, subsidy and control

◘ a private enterprise culture

◘ antagonism of management towards unions.

Continental Europe, in contrast, has:

◘ low autonomy

◘ state and EU intervention

◘ a focus on organisations as partners in social engineering

◘ greater corporate and social responsibilities

◘ the right to employee participation and co-determination.

The nature of these relationships means that managers in the USA have far greater freedom in relation to defining the employment relationship within their organisations. In Europe, the increased role of 'social partners' in the employment relationship means less freedom of action and more difficult hiring and firing decisions.

National business systems

At a broader level, Sparrow and Hiltrop (1994) argue that research in the European context highlights the existence of different systems of business and, indeed, models of capitalism, and that the development and success of specific managerial structures and practices can be explained only with reference to the various institutional contexts within Europe. This is a powerful argument in favour of the need for local responsiveness. Whitley (1992) identifies 16 characteristics of 'national business systems' that together constitute the major dimensions along which comparisons of the nature of management practice should be based (see Box 1).

BOX 1

COMPARATIVE CHARACTERISTICS OF BUSINESS SYSTEMS

The nature of the firm

- the degree to which private managerial hierarchies co-ordinate economic activities
- the degree of managerial discretion from owners
- specialisation of managerial capabilities and activities within authority hierarchies
- the degree to which growth is discontinuous and involves radical changes in skills and activities
- the extent to which risks are managed through mutual dependence with business patterns and employees.

Market organisation

- the extent of long-term co-operative relations between firms within and between sectors
- the significance of intermediaries in the co-ordination of market transactions
- stability, integration and scope of business groups
- dependence of co-operative relations on personal ties and trust.

Authoritative co-ordination and control systems

- integration and interdependence of economic activities
- impersonality of authority and subordination relations
- task, skill and role specialisation and individualisation
- differentiation of authority roles and expertise
- decentralisation of operational control and level of work group autonomy
- distance and superiority of managers
- extent of employer–employee commitment and organisation-based employment systems.

Source: Whitley (1992).

These different configurations represent alternative responses to three fundamental issues:

- how economic activities and resources are controlled and co-ordinated

- how market connections are organised between authoritatively co-ordinated and economic activities

- how activities and skills within firms are organised and directed through authority relations.

A large body of research has considered the impact of national business systems in shaping different managerial practices within Anglo-Saxon and other European national configurations (see for example Kristensen 1992 and Lane 1992). This research provides evidence of significant differences in managerial practices between countries and between groups of countries, although the dynamic nature of national business systems will affect the long-term significance of such groupings.

In summary, research into comparative HRM has shown significant differences at a country level between HR policy and practice, despite the existence of common trends across Europe. This research demonstrates clearly the impact of differing contextual factors at national level, such as political and economic history. It is critical that PM professionals working in international organisations are aware of the nature of such differences, including cultural differences, when making decisions concerning standardised or localised policy and practice.

4 | Approaches to IHRM: HRM in MNEs

◪ **A critical aspect of creating effective international HR strategies is the ability to judge the extent to which an organisation should implement similar practices across the world or adapt them to suit local conditions: the 'global v local' debate.**

◪ **Strategy–structure configurations of international organisations affect the choice of international HRM approach.**

◪ **Work in strategic IHRM has focused on identifying the variables determining strategy choices for international PM professionals.**

The issue of how people management issues should be managed in international companies has been the focus of much interest amongst researchers. The critical question addressed is the need to balance the demands of global integration and local differentiation. This chapter examines first the international business strategy literature and then the strategic international HRM literature to explore the nature of strategic HRM in MNEs.

International business strategy

The ways in which MNEs organise their operations globally has been the subject of extensive research by international management scholars (leading names include Bartlett and Ghoshal 1989; Porter 1990; Prahalad and Doz 1987). A recurrent theme in the literature is the link between strategy–structure configuration in MNEs and the competing demands for global integration and co-ordination or local responsiveness. Where global integration and co-ordination is important, subsidiaries need to be globally integrated with other parts of the organisation and/or strategically co-ordinated by the parent. In contrast, where local responsiveness is important, subsidiaries should have far greater autonomy and there is less need for integration.

Factors influencing the need for integration in global business strategy include:

◪ *Operational integration* – this might be the case in technology-intensive businesses, such as chemicals and pharmaceuticals, where a small number of manufacturing sites can serve wide geographical markets. Equally universal products or markets, such as in the case of consumer electronics, lead to high demands for integration.

◪ *Strategic co-ordination* – organisations can select specific areas where there is a need for centralised management of resources in line with strategy. For instance, significant resources such as research and development may be co-ordinated in terms of strategic direction, pricing and technology transfer, whilst other functions are not.

◪ *Multinational customers* – global competition places a greater demand on co-ordination of resources, both equipment and people. For example, it is important to co-ordinate pricing, service and product support worldwide as a multinational customer can compare prices in different regions.

> **'The competing demands of globalisation and localisation...influence the choice of structure and management control processes within international organisations.'**

Factors influencing the need for differentiation in global business strategy include:

◘ *Market demands* – local responsiveness is more common where local competitors define the market competition, or where products need to be customised to local taste or regulations, such as in the case of processed foods or fashion.

◘ *Legislative demands* – local legislation may prevent full standardisation of services across the globe, leading to a requirement for more tailored approaches.

◘ *Political demands* – barriers to entry in some markets may require an organisation to set up a more autonomous subsidiary primarily staffed by host country nationals (HCNs).

International organisational structures

The competing demands of globalisation and localisation are seen to influence the choice of structure and management control processes within international organisations. There has been much debate about strategy–structure configurations of international organisations amongst both international business and IHRM scholars. A number of typologies of organisational forms have been developed. In general, these typologies denote a move away from hierarchical structures towards network or heterarchical structures.

Hierarchy approaches

Under this form, control rests at the MNE's headquarters, with strong reporting and control systems for subsidiaries. Senior management is composed of parent country nationals (PCNs).

Birkinshaw and Morrison (1995) synthesise earlier work on hierarchical MNE structures to arrive at three basic assumptions underlying these configurations:

◘ Co-ordination costs are economised by grouping tasks according to the geographic or product markets on which they are focused.

◘ Critical resources (including management expertise) are held at the centre to ensure the most efficient use of scarce resources.

◘ The development of an appropriate system to monitor and control divisional managers ensures that the likelihood of opportunistic behaviour on their part is minimised.

Polycentric approaches

Organisations adopting this type of structure reflect less parent control and much greater autonomy of subsidiaries. The term 'multinational' is used by Bartlett and Ghoshal (1986) to define this type of organisation, as it operates in multiple geographic contexts and functions may be duplicated internationally.

Network/heterarchy approaches

In this type of organisation the driving force is to capitalise on the advantages of global spread by having multiple centres. Subsidiary managers are responsible for their own strategy and the corporate-wide strategy. Co-ordination is needed across multiple dimensions (eg functions, products and geography). Each subsidiary is aware of the role of the others; no subsidiary sees itself in isolation from the rest of the global organisation (Hedlund 1986). This type of organisation has been called a *transnational* by Bartlett and Ghoshal

(1987). Transnational organisations aim to develop a truly global culture and mindset amongst their employees.

These typologies developed in the international business strategy literature draw from the seminal work of Perlmutter (1969) and later Heenan and Perlmutter (1979). These writers identified four main approaches to describe how MNEs approach the staffing and management of their subsidiaries. The four categories are:

- *Ethnocentric* – few foreign subsidiaries have any autonomy; strategic decisions are made at headquarters. Key positions at the domestic and foreign operations are held by headquarters' management personnel. In other words, subsidiaries are managed by expatriates from the home country (PCNs). This form of structure and type of control system most closely relates to the hierarchy approaches described above.

- *Polycentric* – the MNE treats each subsidiary as a distinct national entity with some decision-making autonomy. Subsidiaries are usually managed by local nationals (HCNs) who are seldom promoted to positions at headquarters. Likewise, PCNs are rarely transferred to foreign subsidiary operations. This typology relates to the *multinational* type of organisation.

- *Regiocentric* – reflects the geographic strategy and structure of the multinational. Personnel may move outside their countries but only within a particular geographic region. Regional managers may not be promoted to headquarter positions but enjoy a degree of regional autonomy in decision-making.

- *Geocentric* – the MNE takes a worldwide approach to its operations, recognising that each part makes a unique contribution with its unique competence. It is accompanied by a worldwide integrated business and nationality is ignored in favour of ability. PCNs, HCNs and third country nationals (TCNs) can be found in key positions anywhere, including those at the senior management level at headquarters and on the board of directors. This final form of structure and control system relates to the *network/heterarchy* approaches.

Though not without their critics (see for example Mayrhofer and Brewster 1996), these classifications provide indicators for defining the predominant approach to IHRM within an international organisation. The developing field of strategic IHRM has attempted to provide theoretical models to describe the nature of the relationship between HR policy and practice and the strategic orientation of global organisations.

Strategic international HRM

Taylor et al (1996) provide a definition of strategic IHRM derived from the strategic HRM literature:

Strategic Human Resource Management (SHRM)…is used to explicitly link HRM with the strategic management processes of the organisation and to emphasise co-ordination or congruence among the various human resource management practices. Thus, SIHRM (strategic international HRM) is used explicitly to link IHRM with the strategy of the MNC.

Several researchers have proposed detailed models of how IHRM fits into the overall globalisation strategy of organisations. Adler and Ghadar (1990) argue that international organisations go through a series of 'stages' and suggest that organisations will need to follow very different IHRM policies and practices according to the relevant stage of international corporate evolution, which they identify as: domestic, international, multinational and global. Linking this with the attitudes and values of top management at headquarters (using the Heenan and Perlmutter (1979) classifications of ethnocentric, polycentric and geocentric), they outline how organisations could adapt their HRM approaches and practices to fit the external environment in which the firm operates and its strategic intent (see Figure 2).

Schuler *et al* (1993) offer an integrative framework for the study and understanding of strategic IHRM that goes beyond theories of strategic human resource management based in the domestic context and incorporates features unique to the international context. They define strategic IHRM as:

human resource management issues, functions and policies and practices that result from the strategic activities of multinational enterprises and that impact on the international concerns and goals of those enterprises.

Figure 2 | International corporate evolution

	Phase I Domestic	Phase II International	Phase III Multinational	Phase IV Global
Competitive strategy	Domestic	Multidomestic	Multinational	Global
Importance of world business	Marginal	Important	Extremely important	Dominant
Primary orientation	Product or service	Market	Price	Strategy
Product/service	New, unique	More standardised	Completely standardised (commodity)	Mass customised
	Product engineering emphasised	Process engineering emphasised	Engineering not emphasised	Product and process engineering
Technology	Proprietary	Shared	Widely shared	Instantly and extensively shared
Market	Small, domestic	Large, multidomestic	Larger, multinational	Largest, global
Production location	Domestic	Domestic and primary markets	Multinational, least cost	Global, least cost
Structure	Functional divisions	Functional with international division	Multinational lines of business	Global, alliance, heterarchy
	Centralised	Decentralised	Centralised	Centralised and decentralised

Source: Adler and Ghadar (1990)

The breadth of issues is illustrated by the
framework, which links strategic IHRM orientations
and activities to the strategic components of
multinational enterprises (MNEs) comprising inter-
unit linkages and internal operations. These
authors again argue that the key determinant of
effectiveness for MNEs is the extent to which their
various operating units across the world are to be
differentiated and at the same time integrated,
controlled and co-ordinated. Evidence of different
solutions adopted by MNEs to the tension
between differentiation and integration are seen
to result from the influence of a wide variety of
external and internal factors. External factors
include:

◘ industry characteristics such as type of business
and technology available

◘ nature of competitors

◘ extent of change

◘ country/regional characteristics (political,
economic and socio-cultural conditions and
legal requirements).

Internal factors include:

◘ structure of international operations

◘ international orientation of the organisation's
headquarters

◘ competitive strategy

◘ the MNE's experience in managing
international operations.

Figure 3 | Schuler framework

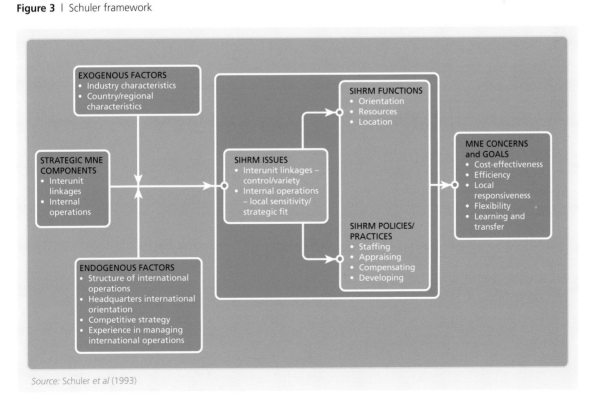

Source: Schuler *et al* (1993)

> **'Rosenzweig and Nohria...argue that of all functions, HRM tends to adhere most closely to local practices, as they are often mandated by local regulation and shaped by strong local conventions.'**

Rosenzweig and Nohria (1994) add to the debate on the tension between pressures for internal consistency and local isomorphism. They argue that of all functions, HRM tends to adhere most closely to local practices, as they are often mandated by local regulation and shaped by strong local conventions. Within HRM they see the order in which six key practices will most closely resemble local practices as:

1   time off

2   benefits

3   gender composition

4   training

5   executive bonus

6   participation.

The underlying assumption for these rankings is that where there are well-defined local norms for the HRM practices and they affect the rank and file of the affiliate organisation, they are likely to conform to practices of local competitors.

Three other factors are identified as being important in determining the extent to which an organisation adopts standard practices worldwide or adapts them to suit local conditions:

1   *Degree to which an affiliate is embedded in the local environment* – this refers to the method of founding and its age, as well as its size, its dependence on local inputs and the degree of influence exerted on it from local institutions.

2   *Strength of flow of resources* – this refers to factors such as capital, information and people between the parent and the affiliate.

3   *Characteristics of the parent* – for example, if the culture of the home country is perceived to be very different from the culture of the subsidiary country, more cultural control will be exercised by headquarters (ie an ethnocentric approach) in order to achieve internal consistency.

Taylor *et al* (1996) apply the resource-based theory of the firm to explain and predict why international organisations adopt different forms of strategic IHRM. The resource-based view suggests that human resource systems can contribute to sustained competitive advantage through facilitating the development of competencies that are firm-specific, produce complex social relationships, are embedded in a firm's history and culture, and generate tacit organisational knowledge (Lado and Wilson 1994).

The model developed identifies the implications of three international HRM orientations to corporate, affiliate and employee group level HR issues, functions, policies and practices:

1   *Adaptive* – under the adaptive approach, affiliate HR systems match the local environment with little control from the parent. (This relates to a polycentric approach.)

2   *Exportive* – the exportive approach is characterised by a replication of parent HR systems in subsidiaries and tight control from headquarters. (This relates to a hierarchical, ethnocentric approach.)

3 *Integrative* – finally, the integrative approach
   seeks to take the best HR systems from
   anywhere in the company and allow for both
   global integration and local differentiation.
   (This relates to a heterarchic, geocentric
   approach.)

This discussion of strategic IHRM demonstrates the
complexity of HR decisions in the international
sphere and the broad scope of its remit – going far
beyond the issue of expatriation, to an overall
concern for managing people effectively on a
global scale. By attempting to adopt a strategic
IHRM perspective, HR practitioners in international
organisations would be engaging in every aspect
of international business strategy and adopting HR
policies and practices aimed at the most effective
use of the human resources in the firm.

5 | The role of the global people management professional

☒ **Historically, the role of the global PM professional focused on the management of expatriates. Managing this group of employees requires a strategic and holistic approach with clear understanding of the role of the host and home country.**

☒ **Problems with expatriation, particularly in relation to work–life balance, have led to the adoption of alternative forms of international working. For organisations, the challenge is to decide which staffing options might best fulfil strategic international operational needs.**

☒ **A key difference between domestic-based and international PM professionals is the complexity involved in operating in different countries and employing different categories of employee.**

Differences between domestic and international HRM activities

The growing interest amongst researchers into theoretical models of strategic IHRM has helped to identify how IHRM differs from HRM in a domestic context on a conceptual level. This analysis does not, however, clarify how the role of an international PM professional differs from domestically based colleagues. Early work defining the nature of IHRM activities focused primarily on the management of expatriates. Morgan (1986), for example, showed how domestic HRM activities change when HRM goes international. His model of international HRM covered three main dimensions:

☒ the three broad human resource activities – procurement, allocation and utilisation

☒ the three national or country categories involved in international HRM activities – the host country where a subsidiary may be located, the home country where the firm is headquartered, and 'other' countries that may be the source of labour or finance

☒ the three types of employee of an international firm – host-country nationals (HCNs), parent-country nationals (PCNs) and third-country nationals (TCNs); thus, for example, a US-based MNE might employ Australian citizens (HCNs) in its Australian operations, send US citizens to Asia-Pacific countries on assignment, and may send some of its Singaporean employees on an assignment to its Japanese operations (as TCNs).

Dowling (1998) provided a summary of the similarities and differences between international and domestic HRM. He attributed the difference to the following six factors:

1   *More HR activities* – to operate in an international environment, the HR function must engage in a number of additional activities such as: international taxation, international relocation and orientation, administrative services for expatriates, host-government relations and language translation services.

' ...because HR managers working in an international environment face...designing and administering programmes for more than one national group of employees, they need to take a broader view...'

2   *The need for a broader perspective* – because HR managers working in an international environment face the problem of designing and administering programmes for more than one national group of employees, they need to take a broader view of issues. For instance, a broader, more international perspective on expatriate benefits would endorse the view that all expatriate employees, regardless of nationality, should receive a foreign service or expatriate premium when working in a foreign location.

3   *More involvement in employees' personal lives* – for employees involved in international transfers, the HR function needs to know more about the employee's personal life to provide the level of support required. This could range from knowing the employee's marital status to providing full pre-departure cultural training for the employee, partner and any dependants. In some organisations, the partner is included in the selection interview, as failure of his or her partner to adapt is the commonest reason for expatriate assignment failure.

4   *Changes in emphasis as the workforce mix of PCNs and HCNs varies* – as the organisation becomes more international, the emphases put on various HR activities change. For instance, if the organisation is adopting a localisation policy, then resources previously allocated to expatriate administration issues may be transferred to activities such as local staff selection, training and management development. A global programme for identifying high-potentials around the world may need to be implemented.

Figure 4 | Model of international HRM

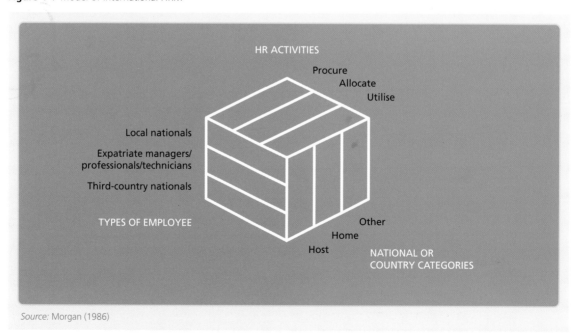

Source: Morgan (1986)

5   *Risk exposure* – the risks involved with failure on international assignments are seen to be more severe than in domestic businesses. The costs of sending someone on an expatriate assignment are estimated to be at least three times' the cost of domestic employment. Indirect costs of a failed assignment may include loss of market share and damage to international customer relationships. In addition to risk of failure, personal security concerns can be extremely high in areas where there is political or civil unrest or a high risk of terrorism.

6   *More external influences* – the global HR function will need to be aware of the type of government, the state of the economy and the generally accepted practices of doing business in each of the various host countries in which the organisation operates. Local labour legislation implications will be especially important in determining the way in which the parent organisation manages its local human resources.

Both of these early descriptions of IHRM reflected a clear focus on expatriation as the key focus of IHR professionals.

The management of expatriates

There has been extensive research into both organisational and individual aspects of expatriation. The strategic management perspective addresses all aspects of the expatriate management cycle (see Figure 5).

In order to adopt a strategic perspective, organisations must first understand the changing context of expatriation. Critical factors here include changes in international organisations,

host locations and the expatriate population itself (Harris and Brewster 1999c).

Changes in international organisations

A number of significant trends can be identified, including the following.

Growth in expatriation in SMEs

In the increasing number of trading blocs throughout the world, and most obviously in the EU, the growth in international business is less amongst the giant 'blue-chips' (which are often reducing their numbers of expatriates) than in smaller or newer organisations in the international arena. These newer organisations will include, for example, some of the giants that privatisation has

Figure 5 | Expatriate management cycle

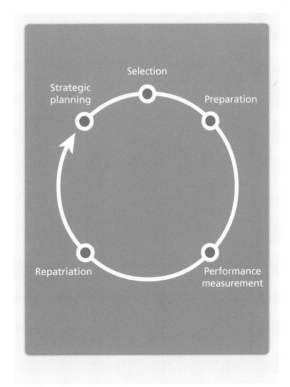

recently freed to compete outside the country of origin. But there are also increasing numbers of small organisations that are beginning to treat the total European market as their own local market. In both cases the experience of internationalisation is limited.

Competitive pressures in MNEs

Amongst the larger and more traditionally international players there have been changes too: a much more competitive environment (D'Aveni 1995) is forcing an increasing attention to cost reduction and cost-effectiveness. Since expatriates are amongst the most expensive people any organisation employs, and the measurement of expatriate performance is, to say the least, uncertain, this has had a direct effect on the way organisations view their expatriates. This has been made more difficult to handle by the reorganisation of MNEs and the consequent reduction in the size of headquarters' operations. Amongst other effects, a move towards organising on the lines of business streams and a reduction in the number of people in corporate international human resource management departments has meant a significant change in the way expatriates are handled. More than a few MNEs have lost the central expertise in the management of expatriates that they had built up over many years.

Growth of expatriation outside the private sector

More and more international governmental and 'non-governmental' organisations, international aid organisations and charities employ more and more international employees. The growth in their work also seems likely to be linked to a growth in expatriation. There has been almost no research into expatriation or the management of expatriates in these non-commercial organisations.

Growth of expatriation in international joint ventures (IJVs) and alliances

The unique issues relating to expatriation in IJVs have only recently been the focus of attention by researchers. Differing forms of control structure and intent in these forms of international organisations create additional complexity for the role of the expatriate.

An IJV is defined as a separate legal organisational entity representing the partial holdings of two or more parent firms, in which the headquarters of at least one is located outside the country of operation of the joint venture. This entity is subject to the joint control of its parent firms, each of which is economically and legally independent of the other (Shenkar and Zeira 1987).

HR issues have been seen to be critical to the successful operation of IJVs. This relates not just to adopting appropriate strategies but also in developing fully trained employees who fit in an IJV's structure and who can manage and implement strategic objectives under the cross-cultural and co-operative management of an IJV (Albrecht *et al* 1996). Many of the failures of IJVs have been attributed to HR issues, such as (Albrecht *et al* 1996):

- staffing

- communication

- delegation of authority from parent firms to the IJV

- difficulties in adapting to a host country.

> '...although organisations are keen to pursue the strategic benefits derived from IJV formation, there is less acknowledgement of the critical impact of HRM in delivering success...'

Lorange (1996) identified and considered five HRM issues within various strategic alliances, including IJVs:

- ◘ assignment of human resources to co-operative ventures (who should be assigned where?)

- ◘ the human resource transferability issue (who 'controls' a particular manager?)

- ◘ the trade-off in time spent between operating and strategic tasks among various managers involved in the venture

- ◘ judgement calls regarding the performance of the human resources in the established venture (how to avoid biases)

- ◘ human resource loyalty issues (to the venture v to the parent).

Albrecht *et al* (1996) argue that, as the key HR issues include selection and recruitment, training and development, spouse and family considerations, performance appraisal, compensation and reward systems, and career and repatriation needs, the HR function should have a critical role when firms decide to enter an IJV.

It is clear that although organisations are keen to pursue the strategic benefits derived from IJV formation, there is less acknowledgement of the critical impact of HRM in delivering success (Cyr and Schneider 1996). According to Cyr (1995), the amount of time spent on HRM issues in IJVs remains small. However, HRM issues in IJVs are very extensive, as we have seen. This apparent dichotomy may be due to the relative paucity of studies related to the development and implementation of HRM practice in IJVs.

Change in host locations

Trends here include:

- ◘ *Fewer expatriates going from the developed world to the developing world* – this is in large part due to increasing unwillingness of the poorer countries to continue taking foreign expatriates instead of using local nationals.

- ◘ *Expatriates moving from the developing world to the developed world* – there has been some increase in expatriates moving in the other direction, as developing countries develop their own international operations.

- ◘ *Expatriates moving between developed countries* – we are witnessing a substantial increase in transfers between developed countries, caused by the extensive European and Japanese investments in the USA and the cross-border developments in new world trading blocs, particularly, of course, in the EU. Figures from Organization Resources Counselors Inc.'s (2000) latest survey of expatriate management trends shows the most popular regional destinations for expatriates as being Asia (33 per cent), Western Europe (26 per cent) and the USA (16 per cent). Expatriate managers working in countries with highly educated and professional employees can no longer adopt an autocratic approach without any regard for the outcomes. Equally, motivation and development of local country nationals is an integral part of creating a truly global operation and as such should be reflected in performance measurement of expatriate managers.

Changes in the expatriate population

The traditional expatriate profile is changing. We are moving away from the career expatriate model, usually filled by white, middle-class, male employees from headquarters. Key features of the expatriate population include:

◘ *More third-country nationals and inpatriates* – as part of a more geocentric staffing policy.

◘ *More women* – although there is still only a small proportion of female expatriates (Adler 1984; Scullion 1994; Harris 1995; Caligiuri and Tung 1998), the number of women expatriates is increasing.

◘ *More dual-career couples* – there have also been dramatic increases in the number of dual-career couples for whom an international assignment presents a series of challenges (Caligiuri and Tung 1998; Harvey 1995, 1996, 1997, 1998; Punnett *et al* 1992; Reynolds and Bennett 1991). Fewer partners, male or female, are prepared to accept a 'trailing' role – not working, but being expected to act as support to their MNE-employed partner and even act as (typically) 'hostess' for corporate functions. Partners now more frequently have their own career or expect to work in the new country.

◘ *Better education levels* – increasing demands for expatriates to deliver value during assignments, linked to the use of expatriate assignments for developmental purposes for high potentials, have resulted in an expatriate population made up substantially of well-educated individuals, with degrees or MBAs.

Strategic planning of expatriation

There is little evidence that expatriate assignments are part of strategic human resource planning on a global scale, except in the case of international management development. Traditionally, expatriates have been sent abroad for the following reasons:

◘ control and co-ordination of operations

◘ transfer of skills and knowledge

◘ managerial development.

In order to operate strategically, organisations need to link foreign assignments more closely to the strategic operational requirements. This requires a careful assessment of whether an expatriate is the best choice in global sourcing decisions. It also implies a need to assess the cost-effectiveness of expatriation. Edwards and Brewster (1996) argue that organisations should adopt a portfolio approach to staffing international assignments. The 'expatriate portfolio' framework allows corporate managers to identify how an international assignment should be managed and whether a local or an expatriate should fill it. The framework outlines four types of assignment based upon the degree of importance of the assignment to the parent organisation and indicates the most suitable type of appointment for each instance. By plotting their assignment against the portfolio, managers can make more rational and sensible sourcing decisions (see Figure 6).

Recruitment and selection

Research into selection criteria for international assignments shows a split between theory and practice. In surveys asking for general views on what makes effective international managers, the criteria mentioned as being critical differ from those reported as being used in practice. The literature on the criteria used for expatriate manager selection also has a tendency towards prescription and a heavy North American bias. There have been several reviews of this literature (Dowling *et al* 1994; Harris and Brewster 1999a).

Phillips (1992) suggests that there is little or no difference between the personal qualities required for success in managing domestic or international business, but successful development of

Figure 6 | The expatriate portfolio

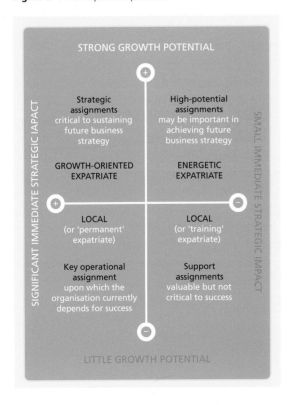

international business demands a higher level of skills and qualities. This is because managers working abroad will be involved in a wider range of activities, roles and responsibilities than those required in the home market. Likewise, Trompenaars (1993) suggests that the international manager has many characteristics of the effective manager operating in a less complex environment. The international manager, however, needs additional skills to reconcile the cultural problems created by the international environment. Possessing an awareness of the difficulties is not enough in this situation.

The similarity between local and international criteria may in some ways be related to the fact that the majority of the studies are not specific in defining the type of expatriate such criteria relate to (Tung 1982). Equally, there is little consideration as to whether criteria will vary according to country, host country role and number of expatriates employed. Forster (1997), however, notes that the many different criteria presented in the literature tend to fall into three broad categories. These are technical competence at work; personality traits/attributes; and interpersonal social skills and personal and family situations.

A study of international managers (not necessarily expatriate managers) revealed clear agreement amongst respondents of attributes that appear desirable whatever the company's strategy. These include (Barham and Devine 1991):

1 strategic awareness

2 adaptability in new situations

3 sensitivity to different cultures

4   ability to work in international teams

5   language skills

6   understanding international marketing.

The list is significant in that four out of the top six characteristics identified represent more 'soft' skills, underlining the human relations aspect of international management and an ability to handle unfamiliar situations.

Coulson-Thomas (1992) asked senior managers in 91 organisations to identify the qualities for effective international operation that are sought in members of a senior management team. Fourteen items were revealed. In order of preference, they were listed as:

◻ strategic awareness

◻ customer focus

◻ individual responsibility

◻ communication skills

◻ creativity

◻ perspective

◻ team player

◻ objectivity

◻ self-discipline

◻ international awareness and perspective

◻ breadth

◻ transnational confidence and effectiveness

◻ European awareness and perspective

◻ language ability.

It is interesting to note that, despite the then imminent establishment of the single European market, these managers were still rating language ability as the least important characteristic of effective international operation.

As a result of interviews with currently operating international managers, Barham and Wills (1992) identified a deeper, core competence, which is essentially holistic in nature, that underpins specific behaviour competencies and skills. The authors labelled this a 'being' competence and split it into three interlinking parts:

◻ *Cognitive complexity* – the ability to perceive several dimensions in a stimulus rather than only one (differentiation), as well as being able to identify multiple relationships among the differentiated characteristics (integration). Features of cognitive complexity include cultural empathy, active listening and a sense of humility.

◻ *Emotional energy* – includes emotional self-awareness, emotional resilience and risk acceptance, together with the emotional support of the family.

◻ *Psychological maturity* – represents managers with a value system that helps them to formulate the dominant goals or themes that make their lives meaningful. Included in this competence is curiosity to learn, a 'present' orientation to time and personal morality.

> '**A key observation from this literature is the emphasis on interpersonal and cross-cultural skills as determinants of success for international assignments.**'

More recently, Birchall *et al* (1996) defined 10 competencies related specifically to the international manager's job. These were:

- global awareness

- international strategy

- international negotiation

- international marketing

- international finance

- cultural empathy

- addressing ethical dilemmas

- building international teams

- working with stakeholders

- foreign language skills.

They asked 102 respondents to rate the competencies on a scale of 1–5, with 5 indicating that the behaviour was of vital importance to successful performance overall. The top five rated competencies as a result of this study were: international negotiation, global awareness, international strategy, international marketing and cultural empathy.

A key observation from this literature is the emphasis on interpersonal and cross-cultural skills as determinants of success for international assignments. The stress on 'soft skills' reflects a more general departure from reliance on traditional 'hard' skills for successful management. A major drawback of these lists, however, is that

few of them are drawn from empirical data. And the tendency is for such lists to end up describing a 'superman' (or less frequently a superwoman). One in-company team of HRM specialists reviewing the range of criteria that have been offered suggested that if they could find a person with all the suggested attributes they wouldn't send them out as an expatriate anywhere – they would make them CEO. However, the gap between theory and practice is so wide as to require a fuller explanation.

Selection criteria in practice

Given the emphasis on interpersonal skills in management theory, it is somewhat surprising to find the research into current practices of MNEs consistently identifies the continuation of more traditional criteria for selection of expatriates.

There appear to be two main findings from the empirical research into selection practices amongst MNEs. The first is that expatriates are selected primarily on the basis of their technical competence alone (see for example Tung 1981, 1982; Zeira and Banai 1984, 1985; Harris 1999). The second finding is that there is an underlying assumption of the universal nature of managerial skills, as first identified by Miller (1973).

The reliance on technical competence may well relate to technical expatriates rather than managerial-level expatriates. However, Miller's (1973) early explanation of companies' preference for technical competence still appears to have relevance today. In his view, companies' perception of international selection as a high-risk operation leads to a tendency to place too much emphasis in recruitment on technical and managerial qualifications, to ensure that the job can be done competently. This view appears to be supported to some extent by subsequent research highlighting the lack of agreement with respect to defining successful performance for expatriate managers and evidence of the resulting general confusion relating to relevant criteria to ensure success. Antal and Izraeli (1993) argue that, in the face of uncertainties about the role of expatriates, the organisational need for certainty in this high-risk area leads managers to select others who are most similar to themselves and, presumably, more likely to be trustworthy and predictable.

Research into actual selection procedures again tends to support Miller's early explanation. Brewster (1991) notes widespread reliance on personal recommendation for expatriate postings from either a specialist personnel staff member or line managers. This results in more or less predetermined selection interviews that consist more of negotiating the terms of the offer than determining the suitability of the candidate. Despite differences in research findings, it would appear that the majority of organisations do not interview the partner and/or family (Bjorkman and Gertsen 1993). Formal testing for potential expatriates is also limited, with restricted use of personality and psychological tests and a general suspicion of the validity of cultural awareness or adaptability tests (Forster 1997; Scullion 1994). In practice, selection for international assignments is often less standardised and more informal than for national appointments (Harris and Brewster 1999a).

Expatriate preparation – adjustment

The ability of expatriates to adjust to their new environment is a critical factor in determining the success or failure of an assignment. The degree to which the individual adjusts is influenced by two issues: the individual's desire to maintain his or her own cultural identity and the extent to which he or she wants to integrate with host nationals. Berry et al (1988) have outlined four different approaches to adjustment:

1 *Assimilation* takes place when the individual wishes to integrate with host nationals and has no desire to maintain his or her own culture.

2 *Integration* occurs when the individual continues to have an interest in his or her own culture whilst also interacting with host nationals.

3 A *separatist* mode of acculturation occurs when individuals want to keep their cultural identity without any desire to integrate with host-country nationals.

4 *Marginalisation* arises when there is no desire to identify with one's own culture or to mix with host nationals.

Marginalisation and separation do not lead to successful expatriate adjustment (DeCieri et al 1991). The most common approach to successful expatriate adjustment is integration.

Research has shown that there are four main groups of variables that seem to affect the adjustment process: individual, job, organisational and non-work variables.

Individual characteristics

◘ *Personal characteristics* – many researchers claim that an individual who is chosen to work on an overseas assignment should possess certain personal characteristics: flexibility, a desire to adjust, tolerance of ambiguity, leadership qualities, interpersonal skills and self-confidence, cultural empathy, emotional stability (Collins 1995; Brewster 1993; Coyle 1992; Hiltrop and Janssens 1990).

- *Language ability* – an individual's desire to learn the host-country language may also influence the adjustment process

- *Previous international experience* – Black and Gregersen (1991) claim that individuals who have previously worked overseas can use their previous adjustment experience to adapt more easily to the new environment. Black and Stephens (1989) found a positive relationship between previous international work experience and work adjustment, but not general adjustment.

Job variables

Five job variables are seen to affect expatriate adjustment, namely: role novelty, role clarity, role discretion, role conflict and role overload.

- *Role novelty* – this reflects the degree of difference between the expatriate's previous position and the new one (Morley *et al* 1997). If the new position is substantially different to the previous position, the expatriate may experience greater feelings of uncertainty and unpredictability.

- *Role ambiguity* – role clarity refers to the extent to which expatriates know what duties they are expected to perform in the overseas assignment. If the role is ambiguous, the expatriate may find it difficult to choose the necessary behaviours, which may cause him or her to feel ineffective and frustrated (Black 1988).

- *Role discretion* – this reflects the expatriate's authority to determine the parameters of the new position. Greater role discretion will enable the expatriate to use past actions that proved effective in a previous role. This should make adjustment easier as it reduces uncertainty and increases the expatriate's confidence in his or her ability to perform in the new environment.

- *Role conflict and overload* – both of these will negatively affect the adjustment of the expatriate. Role conflict takes place when expatriates receive conflicting information about what is expected of them in their new role. Role overload occurs when excessive demands are placed upon the expatriate in the new position.

Organisational variables

Empirical research indicates that certain organisational variables have a significant impact on the expatriate's ability to adjust, namely pre-departure training company support and subsidiary structure (Brewster and Pickard 1994; Macmillan 1991; DeCieri *et al* 1991).

Training

Once an expatriate has been chosen for an overseas position, researchers recommend that MNEs provide formal training for future expatriates and their families. Mendenhall and Oddou (1986) found a positive relationship between training and the expatriate's ability to perform effectively in the foreign environment. Pre-departure training provides the individual with information about the new environment, such as (Mendenhall and Oddou 1986; Tung 1981):

> '...despite the existence of a substantial body of literature and support amongst academic researchers for pre-departure training, research indicates that comparatively little training actually takes place.'

- geography

- housing

- climate

- educational facilities

- cultural orientation

- language training.

Several advantages of pre-departure training have been outlined (Black and Mendenhall 1989):

- it helps to reduce the ill-effects of culture shock

- it reduces the time necessary for expatriate adjustment

- it results in more realistic expectations.

Harris and Brewster (1999b) propose an integrative framework for pre-departure preparation that takes into account job variables at the home- and host-country level, individual variables and an assessment of the individual's existing level of competency before deciding on an appropriate preparation scenario.

However, despite the existence of a substantial body of literature and support amongst academic researchers for pre-departure training, research indicates that comparatively little training actually takes place. Recent surveys by Cendant International Assignment Services (1999) and GMAC GRS/Windham International (2000) found that only half of respondents provided training for international assignees. Even where training was available, the provision was limited to intercultural and language training.

Level of company support

Research indicates that company support has an important impact on the expatriate's ability to adapt to the new environment (Brewster and Scullion 1997; DeCieri et al 1991; Coyle 1992; Hiltrop and Janssens 1990). If there is poor communication between the parent company and the overseas company, an information gap may develop that could result in the expatriate feeling isolated and frustrated. If expatriates fail to receive clear instructions about their new role, this often increases uncertainty and impedes their ability to adapt to the new role. Logistical support such as information on housing, education and travel should help to reduce this uncertainty, thus facilitating adjustment.

Non-work characteristics
Family situation

The inability of the partner and children to adapt to the cultural environment is frequently cited as a common cause of expatriate failure (Jones 1997; Collins 1995; Moore and Punnett 1994). However, the Cendant International Assignment Services 1999 survey revealed that only 41 per cent of organisations formally assess the family's suitability for an international assignment. If a partner or family member is undergoing severe culture shock or experiencing difficulty in making the cross-cultural adjustment, the morale and performance of the expatriate may be adversely affected (Torbiörn 1997). Children are also very resistant to moving due to the educational and social disruption it may cause. Research has shown that the older and greater the number of children, the greater the likelihood of adjustment problems (Church 1982). It would appear that a positive family situation is likely to enhance the expatriate's cross-cultural adjustment and increase the chances of a successful assignment (Collins 1995; Punnett and Ricks 1992).

Cultural novelty

The degree of cultural difference between the home and host country can have a significant influence on the expatriate's ability to adapt. If the host-country culture is very different to the home culture, the expatriate may have to develop a complete set of new behaviours in order to 'make sense' of this new macro-environment and to work successfully in the culture. The expatriate may find it difficult to perceive and learn these behaviours, thus increasing the period of time required for expatriate acculturation.

Performance measurement

Given that expatriates are amongst the most expensive people that an organisation employs, it is surprising how little is known about the assessment of their performance and contribution. Of course, it involves a complex range of issues, and research to date suggests that rigorous performance appraisal systems for expatriates are far from universal (Brewster 1991; Schuler *et al* 1991). The assessment of expatriate performance requires an understanding of the variables that influence an expatriate's success or failure in a foreign assignment. The last section on adjustment has highlighted the critical variables linked to expatriate adjustment. As yet, however, no definitive causal links have been established between adjustment and performance.

An objective appraisal of subsidiary (and expatriate) performance is likely to be highly complex. This may be because of:

◻ conflict between global and subsidiary objectives

◻ non-comparability of data between subsidiaries

◻ volatility and variability of international markets

◻ ambiguity in reporting relationships.

This already problematic relationship is further complicated by the necessity of reconciling the tension between the need for universal appraisal standards with specific objectives in local units. It is also important to recognise that more time may be needed to achieve results in markets that enjoy little supporting infrastructure from the parent company (Schuler *et al* 1991).

Repatriation

The final element in the expatriate management cycle is the repatriation phase. The relationship between the foreign assignment and the future human resource needs of the organisation has become more important with an increasing focus on the need to develop international/global mindsets (Harvey *et al* 1999; Tung 1998) and the role of expatriates as mechanisms of knowledge transfer (Bonache and Brewster 2001). In this respect, evidence of major problems with repatriation for multinational companies is worrying. A survey of 100 multinational companies (Cendant 1999) revealed that although almost 70 per cent had a formal repatriation policy, more than half did not measure or track what happened to assignees on return to their home. Figures from similar surveys (GMAC GRS/Windham International 2000; ORC 2000) suggest that over a quarter of repatriates leave their firms within two years of returning. As nearly half the respondents did not keep records of the career outcomes of repatriates, this figure is likely to be much higher.

> '...findings suggest that organisations should devote more attention to their handling of repatriation and that it should be part of the overall planning of the international assignment.'

BOX 2

Expatriates who were surveyed regarding what companies can do in terms of overseas performance evaluations made the following three points (Oddou and Mendenhall 1991):

1   Modify the normal performance criteria to fit the overseas position and site characteristics. This involves doing an in-depth study of what the key factors of success are for the overseas operation. Once these factors are isolated, the company can use a performance evaluation programme that is designed especially for each subsidiary... . Companies need to pay close attention to the culture of the overseas industry, country and competitor companies when designing strategy and performance measures for their overseas subsidiaries.

2   Include the expatriate's insights as part of the evaluation. The expatriates should have the chance to communicate insights as to how the overseas operation can better co-ordinate with the parent company. For example, if a subsidiary in India needs supplies by specific dates in order to accommodate local laws and customs, passing on the details of the state of affairs to the home office is important... . Whenever expatriate managers are able to iron out such differences, they should be rewarded.

3   Use both the on-site manager and a former expatriate who is now assigned to headquarters to evaluate the expatriate's performance... . These evaluators can act as a check and balance for each other, and both should be educated in the cross-cultural dilemmas regarding the reality of work and life for expatriate managers.

The problem has been emphasised in recent years, particularly in Europe, because the expansion of foreign operations has taken place coincident with a rationalisation of headquarters operations. In the leaner headquarters operations of today's world, there are few spaces for expatriates to 'fill in' whilst the organisation looks for a more permanent position for them. A majority of organisations now do not provide post-assignment guarantees (GMAC GRS/Windham International 2000; ORC 2000). From the repatriate perspective, other problems associated with reintegrating into the home country are (Johnston 1991):

◘ loss of status

◘ loss of autonomy

◘ loss of career direction

◘ feeling that international experience is undervalued by the company.

A critical issue in repatriation is the management of expectations (Pickard 1999; Stroh *et al* 1998; Welch 1998). Work-related expectations of repatriates can include:

◘ job position after repatriation

◘ standard of living

◘ longer-term career prospects

◘ opportunities to utilise skills acquired whilst abroad

◘ support and interest from supervisors and colleagues in the home country.

There are few empirical studies concerning the expectations of repatriates. The ones that have been reported note generally high expectations. One study of British repatriates found that 69 per cent of them expected the return to enhance their career prospects and 55 per cent of them expected their return to be exciting and/or challenging (Pickard 1999). Likewise, a study of US expatriates found a majority to be positive about career development (Tung 1998). In a recent study of the career progress of Finnish expatriates, Suutari and Brewster (2001) note that although the respondents (individual repatriates) reported mainly positive career outcomes, 59 per cent of those who stayed with the same employer had seriously considered leaving. In total, about one-third of the repatriate group had changed their employer. From those, one-third had done so while they were still abroad. The timing indicates that they had changed employer earlier than the average repatriation job negotiations started.

These findings suggest that organisations should devote more attention to their handling of repatriation and that it should be part of the overall planning of the international assignment. Examples of best practice in this area include:

- pre-departure career discussions

- named contact person at the home-country organisation

- mentor at host location

- re-entry counselling

- family repatriation programmes

- employee debriefings

- succession planning.

In a global company with a geocentric approach to staffing, effective handling of all stages of an international assignment is critical to ensure the full utilisation and development of their human resources. Mishandling of returning expatriates means that much critical knowledge is lost to the organisation.

Expatriate failure

This review of the expatriate management cycle has highlighted the problematic nature of expatriation, in particular in respect of the cost of assignments, which are estimated to be on average three to four times' a normal domestic salary (Copeland and Griggs 1985; Hiltrop and Janssens 1990). Expatriate failure rates are usually defined as 'the number of staff who return home before the agreed end of the international assignment because of poor work performance and/or personal problems' (Forster 1997). Turnover rates for US firms have been estimated to lie in the 20 per cent to 50 per cent range for expatriate transfers (Hogan 1990; Harvey *et al* 1999). This figure has been questioned and shown to be exaggerated (Harzing 1995). However, underperformance, which falls short of requiring the expatriate to be brought home, is a more widespread problem (Forster 1997). The cost of expatriate failure extends far beyond the direct costs of salary and relocation expenses and can include:

- lost business

- damaged relationships

- demotivation of the host-country team

'...findings...raise concerns regarding effective management of newer forms of international assignment, such as international commuter and frequent-flyer assignments.'

- personal damage to the expatriate and his or her family.

Organisations are also finding that it is becoming harder to attract individuals to take up long-term international assignments due to a combination of decreasing subsidies and allowances and an increasing number of dual-career couples where the partner is reluctant to sacrifice his or her career.

Managing alternative forms of international working

As a result of the many problems associated with expatriation, it has been argued that organisations will look for alternatives to expatriate assignments. Reducing the amount of international working is, however, not an option. The increasing globalisation of business reinforces the need for control and co-ordination of operations, transfer of skills and knowledge, and development of global managerial competence, all reasons why individuals have traditionally been sent on expatriate assignments (Black *et al* 1992). For organisations the challenge is to decide which staffing options might best fulfil strategic international operational needs. A move away from reliance on long-term assignments increases the complexity of strategic decision-making in this area. IHR professionals now need to decide which type of international assignment might be better for:

- developing an international managerial cadre

- skills and knowledge transfer

- control and co-ordination of operations.

At present, there is little evidence available to assess whether organisations are moving towards new forms of international working and to identify some of the strategic management and personal issues arising from alternative methods of working across borders. A recent survey by CReME (Centre for Research into the Management of Expatriation 2000) provides some empirical data from 60 European organisations with international operations.

The survey findings highlighted that long-term assignments still account for the highest proportion of international working scenarios. Over 53 per cent of respondents had more than 50 employees on long-term assignments as opposed to only 18 per cent for short-term assignments, 6 per cent for international commuters and 26 per cent for frequent flyers. The survey found, however, that organisations appeared to be making increasing use of all four types of international assignment.

The main reasons for using long-term assignments were:

- skill transfer (74 per cent)

- managerial control (62 per cent)

- management development (60 per cent).

For short-term assignments the reasons were:

- skill transfer (69 per cent)

- management development (39 per cent).

International commuting assignments were used mainly for:

◘ skill transfer (32 per cent)

◘ managerial control (25 per cent).

Frequent-flyer assignments were used predominantly for:

◘ managerial control (40 per cent)

◘ skill transfer (26 per cent)

◘ developing an international cadre (20 per cent).

The degree to which the different forms of international working were managed effectively by IHR functions differed dramatically. Although worldwide headquarters HR managers would seem to be the obvious choice for handling policy determination for international assignments, this does not always happen. Whilst most policies for long-term assignments were determined by the headquarters HR department, in the case of short-term assignments this figure was reduced to half and for international commuters and frequent flyers, only a quarter of organisations had a headquarters HR-determined policy.

The problems facing IHR managers trying to manage new forms of international working were highlighted by responses to questions about financial reporting responsibilities. Whilst two-thirds (68 per cent) of the participants prepared a cost analysis for long-term assignments, only half of the companies did so for short-term assignments, approximately a third for international commuters, and less than a fifth knew the costs of frequent-flyer assignments.

Organisations found it harder to identify indirect costs; however, it was clear that alternatives to expatriation were not without problems of their own for both organisations and the individuals concerned.

Critical problems for short-term assignments were seen to be:

◘ work–life balance issues that include long hours on a project and social/family separation

◘ controlling the number of employees

◘ frequent assignment extensions.

In terms of international commuter assignments, the main problems for the individual were:

◘ burnout

◘ travel fatigue

◘ maintaining a balance between work and life

◘ dealing effectively with cultural challenges (few organisations provide cross-cultural training for employees on these types of assignment).

Frequent flyers produced more of a problem, as many companies stated that they were still seeking to identify frequent flyers within their workforce – due to the absence of a policy for this type of international assignment. The problems of frequent flyers were still undefined. However, the research found that many people were struggling to cope with fatigue caused by extensive travelling.

The research highlights that international working in all its forms is on the increase. By its nature, this type of working is more costly and hard to manage for the organisation. However, it is a vital component of organisations' future strategy in this global world. The findings, however, raise concerns regarding effective management of newer forms of international assignment, such as international commuter and frequent-flyer assignments. Organisations have not established appropriate management control systems for these types of assignment. This needs to be addressed to allow IHR managers to make valid judgements about the effectiveness and contribution of these newer forms of international working to overall organisational objectives.

The complexity of IHRM

Pulling all this together, Dowling (1998) re-emphasised the complexity involved in operating in different countries and employing different categories of employee as a key difference between the role of a domestic-based and international people management professional. He also identified four other variables:

1   cultural environment

2   the industry (or industries) with which the multinational is primarily involved

3   extent of reliance of the multinational on its home country domestic market

4   attitudes of senior management – the importance of international operations may be underemphasised if senior management does not have a strong international orientation; in order to achieve Bartlett and Ghoshal's (1989) vision of a transnational mindset amongst top management, it is necessary to have an HR manager who is able to think globally and formulate and implement HR policies that facilitate the development of globally oriented staff.

The IHR professional, therefore, needs to be able to align IHR policy and practice to the varying demands of internal organisational factors and also to competing external factors as described above. It is evident that there is no 'best way' for organisations working across national boundaries, the balance struck between standardisation and differentiation of practices will depend on the unique circumstances of each organisation.

BOX 3

The United Nations Conference on Trade and Development (UNCTAD) includes an index of 'transnationality' in its annual survey of foreign direct investment. The index comprises:

•   an average of ratios of foreign assets to total assets

•   foreign sales to total sales

•   foreign employment to total employment.

Based on this index, the most foreign-oriented multinationals are Thomson Corporation and Seagram Company, both from Canada, with a total transnationality index of 94.6. In Europe, Nestlé and British American Tobacco have transnationality indexes of 94.2 and 91 respectively.

Figure 7 | Index of transnationality

1=Thomson Corporation	Canada	94.6
1=Seagram Company	Canada	94.6
3 Nestlé	Switzerland	94.2
4 British American Tobacco	UK	91.0
5 Holderbanke Financière	Switzerland	90.5
6 Unilever	UK/Netherlands	90.1
7 ABB Asea Brown Boveri	Switzerland	89.1
8 SmithKlineBeecham	UK	82.3
9 Rio Tinto Zinc	UK/Australia	80.4
10 Philips Electronics	Netherlands	77.8

Source: Adapted from World Investment report 2000. UNCTAD. Data for 1999.

This is where the skill of the IHR professional and his or her management team lies, in their ability to read and translate these demands into a coherent set of policies and practices that will work to maximise the human resource contribution across all their operations worldwide. This will entail strategic choices in the areas of recruitment and selection, reward systems (Sparrow 1999; Bradley *et al* 1999), management development and performance management (Lindholm *et al* 1999). This is set within a context of a rapidly changing nature of international operations and international workers.

6 | Measuring the effectiveness of the IHR function

◲ **Most research investigating the link between people management and organisational performance has been in the domestic context.**

◲ **The extra complexity of factors in the international context makes identification of causal linkages particularly difficult.**

◲ **Measures of effectiveness of the global HR function have been developed. In addition, work is currently being carried out to measure the value of international assignments.**

The preceding chapters have outlined the nature of IHRM in organisations and the influences shaping the set of choices that IHR professionals need to make in deciding on appropriate policy and practice. They have also identified how the role of the global PM professional differs from their domestic-based colleagues. This leads us to consider how the effectiveness of the IHR function can be measured.

Measuring effectiveness: domestic-based research

Many researchers are actively investigating the link between people management and organisational performance (for reviews see CIPD 2000; Patterson *et al* 1998; Richardson and Thompson 1999). Guest (1997) rightly points out that there is a lack of definition in much of the research in this area in terms of the theoretical definition of HRM, HR

practices and performance. However, he (Guest 1999) has produced a simple model of HRM and performance (Figure 8).

At present only a limited number of studies have been able to demonstrate a direct causal linkage through all stages of the chain. In the USA, the Sears Employee–Customer–Profit chain (Rucci *et al* 1998) claimed to demonstrate a causal link between employee attitude, customer satisfaction and shareholder value. A study by the IES (1999) in the UK claimed to do the same in a major retail chain. Taking a comparative dimension to this work would involve adding the problems of differing national definitions of performance (see for example the problems the EU has faced in trying to establish common accounting standards) to the existing problems of defining HR practices and particularly best practice.

Figure 8 | Guest model

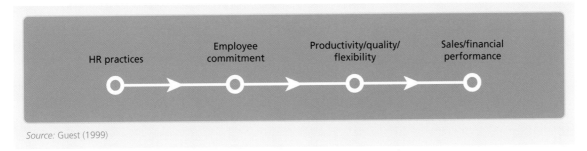

Source: Guest (1999)

> **'For most studies in this area...the key focus is on identifying the type of HR practices adopted and assessing these against published organisational performance figures.'**

For most studies in this area, however, the key focus is on identifying the type of HR practices adopted and assessing these against published organisational performance figures. Three main approaches can be identified in this field of enquiry: the best practice approach, the contingency approach and the configurational approach.

Best practice approach

The *best practice* approach argues that certain HRM practices, or high-performance work systems (HPWS), lead to superior organisational performance. These practices will be the same in any context. The best known proponent of this approach is Pfeffer (1994), who advocates a list of seven HR practices of successful organisations:

- employment security

- selective hiring

- self-managed teams

- high compensation contingent on performance

- training

- reduction of status differentials

- sharing information.

Contingency approach

The *contingency* approach argues that the particular set of HR practices an organisation adopts must fit with other organisational factors to be effective. For example, Schuler and Jackson (1987) identified sets of HR practices that would be appropriate for differing competitive strategies.

Configurational approach

The *configurational* approach emphasises the need to achieve horizontal or internal fit. This involves developing specific, mutually reinforcing combinations of practices that are contingent with organisational circumstances. Proponents of this approach include MacDuffie (1995) and Huselid *et al* (1997), both of whose research showed that certain 'bundles' of HR practices are associated with increases in productivity, sales and profits.

It is noted, however, that virtually all the studies undertaken in the area of measuring people and performance are within the domestic context. From the preceding review of the nature of IHRM and the role of the IHR professional, it becomes immediately apparent that there are multiple complications in trying to provide one common framework for assessing the impact of people management practices on performance in organisations working across national borders.

Measuring effectiveness: the international research

Stroh and Caligiuri (1998) adopted a 'best practice' approach in their survey examining the effectiveness of the global HR function in 60 US multinationals. They asked global HR executives as well as managers of non-HR areas and the CEOs/ business unit executives of the companies to rate the effectiveness of the HR function on the key delivery areas for global HR (as ascertained previously through interviews with 84 HR executives from the 60 firms). These were split between principles that HR departments should implement on an *organisation-wide* basis as follows:

- Position the HR function as a strategic partner in global business.

- Develop global leadership through developmental cross-cultural assignments.

- Foster the global mindset of all employees through training and development.

- Implement formal systems that improve worldwide communication.

- Design and implement an international HR information system (HRIS).

Those that should be implemented within the *human resources function* include:

- Ensure flexibility in all HR programmes and processes.

- Develop relationships with international HR counterparts to encourage information exchange.

- Have ability to express the relative worth of HR programmes in terms of their bottom-line contribution to the organisation.

- Have ability to market HR globally as a source of strategic advantage.

- Encourage the relinquishing of domestic HR power to worldwide HR structure.

The survey findings demonstrated that the global HR executives and the CEO/business unit executives rated the global HR function relatively high, while the executives in the other functional areas rated its effectiveness somewhat low. The relationship between the effectiveness of the

global HR function and firm's performance was also examined through the development of a composite multinational corporation success index of economic variables (return on capital, sales growth, return on equity, profit margin). This showed that three factors were related to bottom-line organisational performance measures. These were:

- developing global leadership through cross-cultural assignments

- making HR a strategic partner in global business

- ensuring flexibility in all HR programmes and processes.

Whilst this is an interesting study, the limitations of the research include a lack of consideration of cross-cultural differences in perception, the lack of detail of actual HR practices and the extent to which these are localised or standardised in each subsidiary, and an assumption of the universality of the 'best practice' approach.

There is a clear need for more work in this area. In particular, a critical issue for global PM professionals will be the need to measure the value of international assignments. Most professionals are aware of the cost of an international assignment, but at present there is no clear methodology for assessing the value of different types and objectives of international assignments.

One current research project (Schiuma *et al* 2001) is developing a methodology for assessing the value of different forms of international assignments. Using a qualitative interviewing methodology, the researchers have identified five strategic reasons that drive the value of international workers. A value driver is defined as any managerial target, process or action that affects the value of a company by an increase of its tangible and/or intangible capital. The five main categories of value drivers are:

◻ professional development

◻ knowledge transfer

◻ fulfilment of scarce skills

◻ control

◻ co-ordination.

Although the value drivers identify the strategic reasons for the use of an international assignment, they do not provide managers with a framework to evaluate the value generated by an international assignment. In order to support managers in assessing the value generated by an assignment, a framework – the expatriate value-added map (EVAM) – has been developed. This tool maps the value areas of a company in which an international assignment can generate value.

Depending on its strategic targets, each assignment can provide value in one or more value areas defined by the EVAM. Through the use of a matrix, the direct impact of the different categories of value drivers on the value areas of an organisation is analysed.

The EVAM allows managers to identify the potential areas of value generation for a company, but does not provide guidance on how to assess the value. For this reason an expatriate value monitor has been developed. It is a measurement framework based on five focus value areas. In each area three categories of indicators are defined in order to provide managers with information about the nature of the value generated by an assignment. Moreover, each category is accompanied by a set of general metrics.

Work on the model is still ongoing but it is argued that this approach will enable global PM professionals to make more valid choices concerning the most effective and efficient use of international workers and assignments.

7 | Conclusions and summary

This review has noted the growth of international business and the impact this has had on the role of the people professional. The movement of goods and money and, most dramatically, the growth of international telecommunications, have significantly affected the development of international markets and the way in which business is conducted throughout the world. However, it is the ability of people to understand and leverage these factors that provides real added value – a point made clearly in the case of international joint ventures, where the evidence is plain that it is the people management issues that so frequently lead to failure. The more positive side of this picture is that effective understanding of national differences will not only avoid problems but can be used to generate highly successful international approaches to doing business around the world, which can be more powerful than mono-cultural team thinking.

The review has shown the development of academic thinking in response to these issues in a range of areas that, in turn, help to focus thinking on the role of the international HRM professional. Thus, the debates and research into national cultural differences, which are now more than a century old, have moved from trying to understand the concept, through trying to analyse its component aspects – usually through the mechanism of exploring national values – to the identification of factors in people management that need to be addressed by organisations operating internationally. Most recently, the research is seeking to link this strand of thinking to the concepts of individual differences and to institutional differences between countries. There are good possibilities now that developments in the field will eventually allow us to understand and then to operate deliberately in multicultural (real or

virtual) workplaces by exploiting the positive power of different national cultures.

The cross-cultural work is already linked with ever-more successful attempts to explore differences in the way different countries manage their human resources. There is now overwhelming evidence that nationality is a primary explanatory variable when examining human resource management. The interlocking of national cultural approaches, legislation, education systems, trade unions and representative structures means that it is not possible, or sensible, to manage people in the same way in every country. Our knowledge of these differences is still limited to the major economies of the world, in general, but is growing apace.

There is already a stream of research looking at how (mainly) MNEs manage their workforces across these different systems. This research is beginning to develop from anecdotal material, through case studies and surveys, to attempts to conceptualise the key issues for management in trying to develop coherent international HRM strategies. Inevitably, there is a lack of coherence between these models at present, and they tend to reflect their national origins, but progress has been made and will continue to be made in this area.

This draws us directly into the role of the people management professional. The need for these professionals to understand the strategic orientation of their organisation and to translate this into appropriate policy and practice takes on additional complexity when working across borders. Global people professionals need to take a holistic stakeholder approach in order to ensure they satisfy the requirements of external stakeholders such as local governments and trade unions whilst maximising the effectiveness of the people within the organisation worldwide. It is likely that, as in other areas of HRM, there will be a range of different roles required from the professional experts here, but there is arguably more pressure for those with international responsibilities to be operating at strategic and policy levels, leaving implementation to local managers. At present the requirements of this role are unclear and are something that will be investigated in the CIPD's follow-on research.

CIPD research project

This report forms part of a major research programme being carried out by the CIPD. The aim of the research is to provide a broad, coherent overview of the field of international human resource management (IHRM) and a detailed, practical analysis of what is needed to be successful in this crucial area of modern management.

The CIPD project is already beginning to outline some of the major constituents of the role of the international practitioner. Later stages of the project will compare them with the expectations of the IHRM professionals in major organisations, examine the present and future demands of their roles, and explore the detail of the operation of these roles and how they change over time in a number of different contexts. On the basis of this knowledge the research will look at the competencies and the processes necessary to drive success for global people professionals. The research aims to provide a new model of global HR that will reflect the critical nature of these two factors.

References

ADLER N. J. (1984)

'Women in international management: where are they?'. *California Management Review*. Vol. 26, No. 4. pp78–89.

ADLER N. J. and GHADAR F. (1990)

'Strategic human resource management: a global perspective'. In Pieper R. (ED.) *Human Resource Management in International Comparison*. Berlin/New York, de Gruyter.

ALBRECHT M. H., PAGANO A. M. and PHOOCHAROON P. (1996)

'International joint ventures: an integrated conceptual model for human resource and business strategies'. *Journal of Euro-Marketing*. Vol. 4, No. 3. pp89–127.

ANTAL A. and IZRAELI D. (1993)

'Women managers from a global perspective: women managers in their international homelands and as expatriates'. In Fagenson E. (ED.) *Women in Management: Trends, issues and challenges in management diversity, women and work*. Newbury Park, Calif., Sage Publications.

BARHAM K. and DEVINE M. (1991)

The Quest for the International Manager: A survey of global human resource strategies. London, Economist Intelligence Unit.

BARHAM K. and WILLS S. (1992)

Management Across Frontiers: Identifying the competences of successful international managers. Berkhamsted, Ashridge Management Research Group and the Foundation for Management Education.

BARTLETT C. A. and GHOSHAL S. (1986)

'Tap your subsidiaries for global reach'. *Harvard Business Review*. Vol. 4, No. 6. pp87–94.

BARTLETT C. A. and GHOSHAL S. (1987)

'Managing across borders: new strategic requirements'. *Sloan Management Review. Vol.* 28, Summer. pp7–17.

BARTLETT C. A. and GHOSHAL S. (1989)

Managing Across Borders: The transnational solution. Boston, Mass., Harvard Business Press.

BERGGREN C. (1992)

Alternatives to Lean Production. Ithaca, New York, ILR Press.

BERRY I., KIM R. and BOSHI P. (1988)

'Psychological acculturation of immigrants'. In Kim Y. and Gudykust W. (EDS) *Cross-Cultural Adaptation: Current approaches*. Newbury Park, Calif., Sage Publications.

BIRCHALL D., HEE T. and GAY K. (1996)

'Competencies for international managers'. *Singapore Institute of Management*. January. pp1–13.

BIRKINSHAW J. M. and MORRISON A. J. (1995)

'Configurations of strategy and structure in subsidiaries of multinational corporations'. *Journal of International Business Studies*. Vol. 4. pp729–53.

BJORKMAN I. and GERTSEN M. (1993)

'Selecting and training Scandinavian expatriates: determinants of corporate practice'. *Scandinavian Journal of Management*. Vol. 9, No. 2. pp145–64.

BLACK J. S. (1988)

'Work role transitions: a study of American expatriate managers in Japan'. *Journal of International Business Studies*. Vol. 30, No. 2. pp119–34.

BLACK J. S. and GREGERSEN H. (1991)

'The right way to manage expats'. *Harvard Business Review*. Vol. 77. March–April.

BLACK J. S. and MENDENHALL M. (1989)

'A practical but theory-based framework for selecting cross-cultural training methods'. *Human Resource Management*.

BLACK J. S., GREGERSEN H. and MENDENHALL M. (1992)

Global Assignments. San Francisco, Jossey-Bass.

BLACK J. S. and STEPHENS G. K. (1989)

'The influence of the spouse on American expatriate adjustment in overseas assignments'. *Journal of Management*. Vol. 15. pp529–44.

BONACHE J. and BREWSTER C. (2001)

'Expatriation: a developing research agenda'. *Thunderbird International Business Review*. Vol. 43, No. 1. pp3–20.

BRADLEY P., HENDRY C. and PERKINS S. (1999)

'Global or multi-local? The significance of international values in reward strategy'. In Brewster C. and Harris H. (EDS) *International HRM: Contemporary issues in Europe*. London, Routledge.

BREWSTER C. (1991)

The Management of Expatriates. London, Kogan Page.

BREWSTER C. (1993)

'The paradox of adjustment: UK and Swedish expatriates in Sweden and the UK'. *Human Resource Management Journal*. Vol. 4, No. 1. pp49–62.

BREWSTER C. (1995)

'National cultures and international management'. In Tyson S. (ED.) *Strategic Prospects for HRM*. London, Institute of Personnel and Development.

BREWSTER C. and BOURNOIS F. (1991)

'A European perspective on HRM'. *Personnel Review*. Vol. 20, No. 6. pp36–40.

BREWSTER C., MAYRHOFER W. and MORLEY M. (2000)

'The concept of strategic European human resource management'. In Brewster C., Mayrhofer W. and Morley M. (EDS) *New Challenges for European Human Resource Management*. London, Macmillan.

BREWSTER C. and PICKARD J. (1994)

'Evaluating expatriate training'. *International Studies of Management and Organisation*. Vol. 24, No. 3. pp18–35.

BREWSTER C., TREGASKIS O., HEGEWISCH A. and MAYNE L. (1996)

'Comparative research in human resource management: a review and an example'. *International Journal of Human Resource Management*. Vol. 7, No. 3. pp585–604.

CALIGIURI P. M. and TUNG R. L. (1998)

'Are masculine cultures female friendly? Male and female expatriates' success in countries differing in work value orientations'. In Hofstede G. (chair) *Masulinity/Femininity as a Cultural Dimension*. Paper presented at the International Congress of the International Association for Cross-Cultural Psychology: The Silver Jubilee Congress. Bellingham, Wash.

CENDANT INTERNATIONAL ASSIGNMENT SERVICES (1999)

Policies and Practices Survey 1999. London.

CENTRE FOR RESEARCH INTO THE MANAGEMENT OF EXPATRIATION (2000)

New Forms of International Working. *Cranfield School of Management Report*. February.

CHILD J. (1981)

'Culture, contingency and capitalism in the cross-national study of organisations'. In Staw B. M. and Cummings L. L. (EDS) *Research in Organisational Behaviour*. Vol. 3. pp303–56.

CHURCH A. (1982)

'Sojourner adjustment'. *Psychological Bulletin*. Vol. 91, No. 3. pp540–72.

CIPD (2000)

The Case for Good People Managment: A summary of the research. London, CIPD.

COLLINS S. (1995)

Expatriation: A moving experience. Dublin, Michael Smurfit Graduate School of Business.

COPELAND L. and GRIGGS L. (1985)

Going International. New York, Random House.

COULSON-THOMAS C. (1992)

Creating the Global Company. Maidenhead, McGraw-Hill.

COYLE W. (1992)

International Relocation. Oxford, Butterworth-Heineman.

CYR D. (1995)

The Human Resource Challenge of International Joint Ventures. Westport, Conn., Quorum Books.

CYR D. and SCHNEIDER S. (1996)

'Implications for learning: human resource management in east-west joint ventures'. *Organization Studies*. Vol. 17, No. 2. pp201–26.

D'AVENI R. A. (1995)

Hyper-Competitive Rivalries: Competing in highly dynamic environments. New York, Free Press.

DECIERI H., DOWLING P. and TAYLOR K. (1991)

'The psychological impact of expatriate relocation on partners'. *International Journal of Human Resource Management*. Vol. 2, No. 3. pp377–415.

DOWLING P. J. (1998)

Completing the Puzzle: Issues in the development of the field of international human resource management. Paper presented at the Sixth International HRM Conference. University of Paderborn. June.

DOWLING P. J., WELCH D. and SCHULER R. S. (1994)

International Dimensions of Human Resource Management. Cincinnati, Ohio, South-Western.

EDWARDS C. and BREWSTER C. (1996)

Do You Need Expatriates? Paper presented at IHRM Conference. San Diego. 24–28 June.

FORSTER N. (1997)

'The persistent myth of high expatriate failure rates: a reappraisal'. *International Journal of Human Resource Management*. Vol. 3, No. 4. pp414–34.

GMAC GLOBAL RELOCATION SERVICES/WINDHAM INTERNATIONAL (2000)

Global Relocation Trends 2000 Survey Report. New York.

GUEST D. (1997)

'Human resource management and performance: a review and research agenda'. *International Journal of Human Resource Management*. Vol. 8, No. 3. pp263–76.

GUEST D. (1999)

Do People Strategies Really Enhance Business Success and if so, Why Don't More People Use Them? Presentation at IPD National Conference. Harrogate. October.

HARRIS H. (1995)

'Women's role in international management'. In Harzing A. W. K. and Van Ruysseveldt J. (EDS) *International Human Resource Management*. London, Sage Publications .

HARRIS H. (1999)

'Women in international management: why are they not selected?' In Brewster C. and Harris H. (EDS) *International HRM: Contemporary issues in Europe*. London, Routledge.

HARRIS H. and BREWSTER C. (1999a)

'The coffee machine system: how international selection really works'. *International Journal of Human Resource Management*. Vol. 10, No. 3. June. pp488–500.

HARRIS H. and BREWSTER C. (1999b)

'A framework for pre-departure preparation'. In Brewster C. and Harris H. (EDS) *International HRM: Contemporary issues in Europe*. London, Routledge.

HARRIS H. and BREWSTER C. (1999c)

'International HRM: The European contribution'. In Brewster C. and Harris H. (EDS) *International HRM: Contemporary issues in Europe*. London, Routledge.

HARVEY M. (1989)

'Repatriation of corporate executives: an empirical study'. *Journal of International Business Studies*. Spring. pp131–44.

HARVEY M. (1995)

'The impact of dual-career families on international relocations'. *Human Resources Management Review*. Vol. 5, No. 3. pp223–44.

HARVEY M. (1996)

'Addressing the dual-career expatriation dilemma in international relocation'. *Human Resource Planning*. Vol. 19, No. 4.

HARVEY M. (1997)

'Dual-career expatriates: expectations, adjustment and satisfaction with international relocation'. *Journal of International Business Studies*. Vol. 28, No. 3. pp627–57.

HARVEY M. (1998)

'Dual-career couples during international relocation: the trailing spouse'. *International Journal of Human Resource Management*. Vol. 9, No. 2. pp309–22.

HARVEY M., SPEIER C. and NOVICEVIC M. M. (1999)

'The role of inpatriation in global staffing'. *International Journal of Human Resource Management*. Vol. 10, No. 3. pp459–76.

HARZING A. W. K. (1995)

'The persistent myth of high expatriate failure rates'. *International Journal of Human Resource Management*. Vol. 6, No. 2. pp457–75.

HEDLUND G. (1986)

'The hypermodern MNC – a heterarchy?'. *Human Resource Management*. Vol. 25, No. 1. pp9–35.

HEENAN D. A. and PERLMUTTER H. V. (1979)

Multinational Organizational Development: A social architectural approach. Reading, Mass., Addison-Wesley.

HILTROP J. and JANSSENS M. (1990)

'Expatriation: challenges and recommendations'. *European Management Journal*. Vol. 8, No. 1. March.

HOFSTEDE G. (1980)

Culture's Consequences: International differences in work-related values. London, Sage Publications.

HOFSTEDE G. (1991)

Cultures and Organizations: Software of the mind. London, McGraw-Hill.

HOGAN G. (1990)

'The key to expatriate success'. *Training and Development Journal*. January.

HUSELID M. (1995)

'The impact of human resource management practices on turnover, productivity and corporate financial performance'. *Academy of Management Journal*. Vol. 38. pp635–72.

HUSELID M. A., JACKSON S. E. and SCHULER R. S. (1997)

'Technical and strategic human resource management effectiveness as determinants of firm performance'. Academy of Management Journal. Vol. 40, No. 1. pp171–88.

IES (1999)

From People to Profits. Report 355. Brighton, Institute of Employment Studies.

JOHNSTON J. (1991)

'An empirical study of repatriation of managers in UK multinationals'. *Human Resource Management Journal.* Vol. 1, No. 4. pp102–108.

JONES B. (1997)

'Getting ahead in Switzerland'. *Management Review.* Vol. 86, No. 6. pp58–61.

JOYNT P. and MORTON B. (1999)

The Global HR Manager. London, Institute of Personnel and Development.

KERN H. and SCHUMANN M. (1984)

'New concepts of production in German plants'. In Katzentstein P. J. (ED.) *Industry and Politics in West Germany: Toward the third West German Republic.* Cornell, Cornell University Press.

KLUCKHOLN F. F. and STRODTBECK F. L. (1961)

Variations in Value Orientations. New York, Row, Peterson and Co.

KRISTENSEN P. H. (1992)

'Strategies against structure: institutions and economic organization in Denmark'. In Whitley R. D. (ED.) *European Business Systems: Firms and markets in their national contexts.* London, Sage Publications.

LADO A. A. and WILSON M. C. (1994)

'HR systems and sustained competitive advantage'. *Academy of Management Review.* Vol. 19. pp699–727.

LAMMERS C. J. and HICKSON D. (EDS) (1979)

Organizations Alike and Unlike. London, Routledge and Kegan Paul.

LANE C. (1989)

Management and Labour in Europe. Aldershot, Edward Elgar.

LANE C. (1992)

'European business systems: Britain and Germany compared'. In Whitley R. D. (ED.) *European Business Systems: Firms and markets in their national contexts.* London, Sage Publications.

LAURENT A. (1986)

'The cross-cultural puzzle of international human resource management'. *Human Resource Management.* Vol. 25, No. 1. pp91–102.

LINDHOLM N., TAHVANAINEN M. and BJORKMAN I. (1999)

'Performance appraisal of host country employees in Western MNEs in China'. In Brewster C. and Harris H. (EDS) *International HRM: Contemporary issues in Europe.* London, Routledge.

LORANGE P. (1996)

'A strategic human resource perspective applied to multinational co-operative ventures: the human side of strategic change'. *International Studies of Management and Organisation.* Vol. 26, No. 1. pp87–103.

MACDUFFIE J. P. (1995)

'Human resource bundles and manufacturing performance: organizational logic and flexible production systems in the world auto industry'. *Industrial and Labor Relations Review.* No. 48. pp197–221.

MACMILLAN C. (1991)

'Foreign direct investment flows to Eastern Europe and their implications for developing countries'. *Journal of International Studies.* Vol. 20, No. 2.

MAYRHOFER W. and BREWSTER C. (1996)

'In praise of ethnocentricity'. *International Executive.* Vol. 38, No. 6. November. pp749–78.

MENDENHALL M. E. and ODDOU G. (1986)

'Acculturation profiles of expatriate managers: implications for cross-cultural training programs'. *Columbia Journal of World Business.* pp73–9.

MENDENHALL M. E. and ODDOU G. (1991)

International Human Resources Management. Boston, Mass., PWS-Kent.

MILES R. and SNOW C. (1986)

'Designing strategic human resource systems'. *Organizational Dynamics.* Vol. 12, No. 2. pp36–52.

MILLER E. L. (1973)

'The international selection decision: a study of some dimensions of managerial behaviour in the selection decision process'. *Academy of Management Journal.* Vol. 16, No. 2. pp239–52.

MOORE S. and PUNNETT J. (1994)

'Expatriates and their spouses: a pilot study in the Limerick region and directions for future research'. *Irish Business and Administration Research.* Vol. 15. pp178–84.

MORGAN P. V. (1986)

'International human resource management: fact or fiction'. *Personnel Administrator.* Vol. 31, No. 9. p44.

MORLEY M., BURKE C. and FINN G. (1997)

'The Irish in Moscow: a question of adjustment'. *Human Resource Management Journal.* Vol. 7, No. 3. pp53–67.

ODDOU G. and MENDENHALL M. (1991)

'Succession planning in the 21st century: how well are we grooming our future business leaders?'. *Business Horizons.* Vol. 34, No. 1. Jan–Feb. pp26–34.

ORGANIZATION RESOURCES COUNSELORS INC. (2000)

2000 Worldwide Survey of International Assignment Policies and Practices. London and New York, ORC.

OUCHI W. G. (1981)

Theory Z: How American business can meet the Japanese challenge. New York, Avon Books.

PASCALE R. T. and ATHOS A. G. (1982)

The Art of Japanese Management. London, Allen Lane.

PATTERSON M. G., WEST M. A., LAWTHOM R. and NICKELL S. (1998)

The Impact of People Management Practices on Business Performance. London, Institute of Personnel and Development.

PERLMUTTER M. V. (1969)

'The tortuous evolution of the multinational corporation'. *Columbia Journal of World Business.* Jan–Feb. pp9–18.

PFEFFER J. (1994)

Competitive Advantage Through People. Boston, Mass., Harvard Business School Press.

PHILLIPS N. (1992)

'Cross-cultural training'. *Journal of European Industrial Training.* Vol. 17, No. 2.

PICKARD J. (1999)

Successful Repatriation: Organisational and individual perspectives. PhD Thesis, Cranfield University.

PORTER M. E. (1990)

The Competitive Advantage of Nations. London, Macmillan.

PRAHALAD C. K. and DOZ Y. (1987)

The Multinational Mission: Balancing local demands and global vision. New York, Free Press.

PUNNETT B. J., CROCKER O. and STEVENS M. (1992)

'The challenge for women expatriates and spouses: some empirical evidence'. *International Journal of Human Resource Management.* Vol. 3, No. 3. pp585–92.

PUNNETT B. J. and RICKS D. A. (1992)

International Business. Boston, Mass., PWS-Kent.

REYNOLDS C. and BENNETT R. (1991)

'The career couple challenge'. *Personnel Journal.* March.

RICHARDSON R. and THOMPSON M. (1999)

The Impact of People Management Practices on Business Performance: A literature review. London, Institute of Personnel and Development.

ROSENZWEIG P. and NOHRIA N. (1994)

'Influences of human resource management practices in multinational firms'. *Journal of International Business Studies.* Vol. 20, No. 2. pp229–52.

RUCCI A. J., KIRN S. P. and QUINN R. T. (1998)

'The employee-customer-profit chain at Sears'. *Harvard Business Review.* Vol. 76, No. 1. pp83–97.

SCHIUMA G., BOURNE M., NEELY A. and HARRIS H. (2001)

Assessing the Value of International Assignments. Cranfield School of Management Report. Cranfield.

SCHNEIDER S. (1988)

'National vs corporate culture: implications for human resource management'. *Human Resource Management.* Vol. 27, No. 2. pp231–46.

SCHULER R. S., DOWLING P. J. and DECIERI H. (1993)

'An integrative framework of strategic international human resource management'. *Journal of Management.* Vol. 19, No. 2. pp419–59.

SCHULER R. S., FULKERSON J. R. and DOWLING P. J. (1991).

'Strategic performance measurement and management in multinational corporations'. *Human Resource Management.* Vol. 30. pp365–92.

SCHULER R. S. and JACKSON S. E. (1987)

'Linking competitive strategy and human resource management practices'. *Academy of Management Executive.* Vol. 3, No. 1. pp207–19.

SCULLION H. (1994)

'Creating international managers: recruitment and development issues'. In Kirkbride P. (ED.) *Human Resource Management in Europe.* London, Routledge.

SELS A. (1992)

'The rule of pragmatism in a diverse culture: personnel management in Belgium'. *Personnel Management.* Vol. 24, No. 11. pp46–52.

SHENKAR O. and ZEIRA Y. (1987)

'HRM in international joint ventures: directions for research'. *Academy of Management Review.* Vol. 12, No. 3. pp546–57.

SPARROW P. (1999)

'International reward systems: to converge or not to converge?'. In Brewster C. and Harris H. (EDS) *International HRM: Contemporary issues in Europe.* London, Routledge.

SPARROW P. and HILTROP J. M. (1994)

European Human Resource Management in Transition. Hemel Hempstead, Prentice-Hall.

STROH L. K. and CALIGIURI P. (1998)

'Increasing global effectiveness through effective people management'. *Journal of World Business.* Vol. 33, No. 1. pp1–17.

STROH L. K., GREGERSEN H. B. and BLACK J. S. (1998)

'Closing the gap: expectations versus reality among expatriates'. *Journal of World Business.* Vol. 33, No. 2. pp11–124.

SUUTARI V. and BREWSTER C. (2000)

'Making their own way: international experience through self-initiated foreign assignments'. *Journal of World Business.* Vol. 35, No. 4. pp417–36.

SUUTARI V. and BREWSTER C. (2001)

'Repatriation: empirical evidence from a longitudinal study of careers and expectations among Finnish expatriates'. *International Journal of Human Resource Management.*

TAYLOR S., BEECHLER S. and NAPIER N. (1996)

'Towards an integrative model of strategic international human resource management'. *Academy of Management Review.* Vol. 21, No. 4. pp959–65.

TORBIÖRN I. (1997)

'Staffing for international operations'. *Human Resource Management Journal.* Vol. 7, No. 3.

TROMPENAARS F. (1993)

Riding the Waves of Culture: Understanding cultural diversity in business. London, Economist Books.

TUNG R. L. (1981)

'Selection and training of personnel for overseas assignments'. *Columbia Journal of World Business.* Vol. 16, No. 1. pp68–78.

TUNG R. L. (1982)

'Selection and training procedures of US, European and Japanese multinationals'. *California Management Review.* Vol. 25, No. 1. pp57–71.

TUNG R. L. (1998)

'American expatriates abroad: from neophytes to cosmopolitans'. *Journal of World Business.* Vol. 33, No. 2. pp125–44.

ULRICH D. (1987)

'Organizational capability as competitive advantage: human resource professionals as strategic partners'. *Human Resource Planning.* Vol. 10. pp169–84.

VAILL P. (1989)

Managing as a Performing Art: New ideas for a world of chaotic change. San Francisco, Jossey-Bass.

WELCH D. (1998)

The Psychological Contract and Expatriation: A disturbing issue for IHRM? Paper presented at Sixth Conference on International Human Resource Management. University of Paderborn. 22–25 June.

WHITLEY R. D. (1992)

European Business Systems: Firms and markets in their national contexts. London, Sage Publications.

WRIGHT P. M. and MCMAHAN G. C. (1992)

'Theoretical perspectives for strategic human resource management'. *Journal of Management.* Vol. 18, No. 2.

ZEIRA Y. and BANAI M. (1984)

'Selection of expatriate managers in MNEs: the lost environment point of view'. *International Studies of Management and Organisation.* Vol. 15, No. 1. pp33–51.

ZEIRA Y. and BANAI M. (1985)

'Present and desired methods of selecting expatriate managers for international assignments'. *Personnel Review.* Vol. 13, No. 3. pp29–35.